EMIL AND KATHLEEN SICK SERIES
IN WESTERN HISTORY AND BIOGRAPHY

With support from the Center for the Study of the Pacific Northwest at the University of Washington, the Sick Series in Western History and Biography features scholarly books on the peoples and issues that have defined and shaped the American West. Through intellectually challenging and engaging books of general interest, the series seeks to deepen and expand our understanding of the American West as a region and its role in the making of the United States and the modern world.

DIANA L. DI STEFANO

ENCOUNTERS *in*
AVALANCHE COUNTRY

A History of Survival in the Mountain West, 1820–1920

CENTER FOR THE STUDY
OF THE PACIFIC NORTHWEST

in association with

UNIVERSITY OF WASHINGTON PRESS
Seattle and London

CENTER FOR THE STUDY OF THE PACIFIC NORTHWEST
PO BOX 353587, SEATTLE, WA 98195, USA

UNIVERSITY OF WASHINGTON PRESS
PO BOX 50096, SEATTLE, WA 98145, USA
www.washington.edu/uwpress

Library of Congress Cataloging-in-Publication Data
Di Stefano, Diana L.
   Encounters in avalanche country : a history of survival in the Mountain West, 1820–1920 / Diana L. Di Stefano.
      pages   cm. — (Emil and Kathleen Sick series in Western history and biography)
   Includes bibliographical references and index.
   ISBN 978-0-295-99314-0 (hardback)
   1. Frontier and pioneer life—West (U.S.)   2. Frontier and pioneer life—Rocky Mountains.   3. Mountain life—West (U.S.).   4. Mountain life—Rocky Mountains.   5. Avalanches—West (U.S.)—History.   6. Avalanches—Social aspects—West (U.S.)—History.   7. Avalanches—Rocky Mountains—History.   8. Avalanches—Social aspects—Rocky Mountains—History.   9. Human ecology—West (U.S.)—History.   10. Human ecology—Rocky Mountains Region—History.   I. Title.
   F596.D5   2013
   978'.02—dc23   2013027325

To my family and the memory of my mother,

Joan Elisabeth DiStefano

CONTENTS

ACKNOWLEDGMENTS

I OWE THE COMPLETION OF THIS BOOK TO THE SUPPORT OF MY MEN-
tors, colleagues, and employers. Donna Krasnow's and Bob Walch's teaching skills gave me the foundation to pursue both history and writing. Anne
Hyde, Betsy Jameson, and Carol Neel remain valued mentors and friends.
At the University of Montana, Dan Flores and Dave Emmons inspired my
intellectual growth. Dan has continued to be an indispensable critic and
supporter of my work. At the University of Colorado in Boulder, I learned
about the craft of history from Virginia Anderson, Bob Ferry, Julie Greene,
Nan Goodman, Ralph Mann, Mark Pittenger, and Carolyn Ramsey. I owe a
special debt to Peter Boag, my dissertation adviser. I will always be grateful
for his insistence on solid evidence, organized writing, and analytical rigor.
My amazing cohorts at Colorado, John Enyeart, John Grider, Beth Kovacs,
Eric Morgan, Wendy Rex-Atzet, Duke Richey, and Allison Wickens, all
offered insightful input. My colleagues at Pacific Lutheran University, Bucknell University, and University of Alaska–Fairbanks offered impromptu
advice and support. I am grateful for the curiosity and good humor of my
students at those institutions as well. Parts of the book appeared in *Journal
of Social History* and *Environmental History*, and I thank those publications
for their permission to rework the material here. Appreciation, too, goes
to my graduate assistant Matt Robinson and map maker Kerri Crowder. I
also owe thanks to Laura Avedisian, Lincoln Bramwell, Doug Smith, and
Leon Unruh; my anonymous reviewers; and my readers at the University of
Washington Press for their patience looking through my manuscript.

This book was possible due to funding from the University of Colorado,
the Charles Redd Center for Western History, and Bucknell University.
Due to the generosity of these institutions, I was able to pursue research at
Denver Public Library, Glenbow Archives, Parks Canada Archives in Rev-
elstoke, Revelstoke Museum and Archives, Revelstoke Railway Museum,
Stephen H. Hart Library at the Colorado Historical Society, University of

Utah Archives, and Utah Historical Society, Washington State University Archives and Special Collections, the Washington State Archives, and the Wenatchee Valley Museum and Archives. Gary Krist generously shared his sources related to the Wellington slide with me.

This book would not have happened without the emotional, intellectual, and financial support of my friends and family. I am privileged to have too many friends to list them all by name, but their faith in my work has been invaluable. My father Lew's love of the West, a passion he passed on to me, inspired this book. My sister Anne Marie's excellent editing and listening skills motivated me through the difficult times. My loyal canine companions, Skaia and Emma, reminded me that walks are important, too. Finally, the memory of my mother's resilient spirit has sustained me.

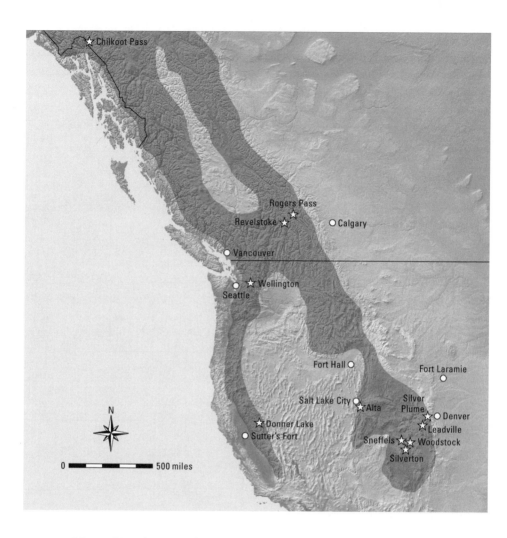

Western United States and Canada with study areas in Avalanche Country shown.

ENCOUNTERS IN AVALANCHE COUNTRY

INTRODUCTION:
ARRIVAL IN AVALANCHE COUNTRY

D R. CHARLES FOX GARDINER FOUND HIS FIRST DAY IN THE MOUN-
tains fundamentally strange. A self-described "tenderfoot," Gardiner
arrived in Crested Butte, Colorado, in the 1880s. As he walked toward
his hotel, the towering mountains, deep snow, thin air, and residents skiing about made an immediate impression. Then he "heard a distant rum-
ble that sounded like thunder in the mountains; it grew heavier, the walk
under ... [his] ... feet shook, and then, with a last roar, the sound stopped."
He remembered, "No one on the walk seemed to notice it so I asked a passing miner" what had happened. The miner replied, "'Why, man alive ...
don't you know snowslides when you hear them?'" This first encounter
with the "growl of the mountain giant that strikes terror to those ... in its
path" reinforced for Gardiner the fact that he had come to a place quite
different from the home he had left in New York.[1]

Over the years Gardiner spent in the Elkhorn Range, he would become
better acquainted with avalanches, or snowslides—as the miners called
them—and make many adjustments to practice medicine in his new home.
He would learn to ski, which was the only way to reach patients in the
wintertime, and to treat maladies like snow blindness—temporary loss of
sight caused by the sun's reflection off the snow. And like others before and
after him, he would discover that the process of community building in a
mountainous environment demanded he cope with extremes of climate
and topography. Gardiner had arrived in what is known today as Avalanche Country, places where steep slopes and snow converge with deadly
potential.

The conditions that lead to avalanches begin with snowflake structure. Snowflakes form many shapes—the more complex the shape, the
more tightly the ice crystals bond together on the ground. Temperature,

moisture content, wind speed, and melting and refreezing rate also affect bonding. Snow falls; layers build. Avalanches occur most often on slopes between 30 to 60 degrees, when the weight of new snow breaks the bonds between the underlying layers.

Two of the most common types of avalanches are loose snow and slab avalanches. A loose snow avalanche begins at a single point at the top of a ridge and as it streaks downhill it destabilizes the surface snow in its path, which then becomes part of the slide. This kind of slide often follows creek beds or gullies and tends to recur, following the same path year after year. Slab avalanches begin when a crack, perpendicular to the fall line, forms between snow layers. The mass of unstable snow breaks off along the crack and moves downhill; slab avalanches can comprise huge amounts of snow, move up to 200 miles per hour, and are less predictable than loose snow slides.

Several factors make regions within the Mountain West particularly prone to avalanche activity. In southwestern Colorado, for example, the San Juan Mountains are extraordinarily steep and receive a fair amount of sun in the wintertime. This creates particularly hazardous snow conditions, because the sun melts both surface and subsurface layers of snow, which then refreeze at night. This cycle produces unstable snow layers with poor cohesion. As a result, the snow cover of the San Juan region has an extremely unstable stratigraphy, which means that the layers are more likely to slip off one another on steep slopes, creating an avalanche.[2] The Cascades in Washington also experience frequent slides. They are also steep, but receive massive amounts of wet, heavy snow—averaging nearly thirty-eight feet during the winter. Changes in the rate of snowfall, temperature fluctuations that mean it can rain and snow during the same storm, alterations in wind speed, and variations in the density of the snowpack contribute to conditions that increase the likelihood of slides.[3]

Those with avalanche experience argue that where slides have fallen once, they are likely to occur again. This belief influences modern avalanche-control methods on highways and at ski resorts where artillery and dynamite are used to stimulate slides before catastrophic amounts of snow have accumulated. Over time, avalanche science has become a respected field of study; manuals advise backcountry users how to avoid risk; and technological advances like avalanche radio beacons, a device worn by skiers that emits a tracking signal, improve chances of survival for victims buried in slides. Nevertheless, deadly disasters occur every year. The number of deaths in avalanches has hovered around twenty to thirty a year in North America in recent decades. Most who died were recreationists: snow machine riders and backcountry skiers.

In the nineteenth century, well before mountains became risky places to play, Americans saw them as obstacles to western expansion. Exploration of the Mountain West by European Americans yielded strong reactions that would seem to prohibit settlement. After traveling through southwestern Colorado's San Juan Mountains, which included hundreds of peaks that tower more than 13,000 feet, John C. Frémont declared the range "one of the highest, most rugged, and impracticable of all the Rocky Mountain ranges, inaccessible to trappers and hunters even in summer."[4] Guidebook writer Lansford W. Hastings wrote in 1845 that the Rocky Mountain range "is usually covered with perpetual snow." The "greatest elevations in all Oregon [Territory], are found in this range, many of which are more than 25,000 feet above the level of the sea. . . . From the foregoing remarks, and from the well-known fact, of the entire sterility of all this range, it will be readily seen, that it is no wise, adapted to the support of man or beast."[5] Hastings was similarly impressed by the Cascade Range in Washington. He estimated they stretched "from twelve to eighteen thousand feet" into the sky.[6] The twelve volcanic peaks were formidable, and "wherever you are [in the region], you behold these ancient pyramids of eternal ice and snow, . . . amid the howling tempest, the flashing lightnings, and the roaring thunders above."[7] Perhaps Hastings portrayed the mountains in this awe-inspiring way to encourage settlers to hasten toward the coast, but his descriptions of "eternal snow" and "extraordinary altitude and sterility" sent a striking message about the hostility of the western mountains.[8]

Now we know that Hastings was somewhat off the mark; the highest peak in the Rocky Mountains, Mount Elbert, stands 14,433 feet. More than fifty other peaks in Colorado surpass 14,000 feet but reach nowhere near the heights he estimated. The highest mountain in the Cascades is Mount Rainier at 14,410 feet, and the highest mountain in the contiguous United States, Mount Whitney at 14,505 feet, is in the Sierra Nevada. In spite of Hastings's inaccurate estimations, these three towering mountain ranges, young in geological terms, left a mark on the trappers, emigrants, and prospectors who traversed them, particularly during the winter season, which could last as long as nine months.[9]

By the second half of the nineteenth century the mountains' raw materials—gold, silver, copper, coal, and timber—funded and fueled eastern development.[10] The mountain ranges had become more than areas to map or cross; they became places to build communities. The search for gold and silver, especially, drove people higher into the mountains, and some of the most productive mines in the region, such as Leadville, Colorado, sat above 10,000 feet.[11]

Prospecting and placer mining came first, but the real riches lay underground and demanded capital investment to extract. Rail lines and spur routes brought in the equipment for underground mining and provided a way to export the ore. The process of developing corporate mines, which depended on the railways, happened at different rates of speed and at different times, but by the end of the nineteenth century many sites in the West had made the transition to company-run mines that employed dozens or even hundreds of workers. In the span of a few decades, more and more people moved into the West; railroads crisscrossed the landscape; and industrial mining, logging, farming, and cattle ranching characterized the economy.

By 1880, "the West had become the most urbanized region in the United States."[12] The buffalo—a symbol of the American West and the native way of life—were almost gone, hunted to near extinction and their bones left to bleach in the sun by market hunters. Livestock owners and bounty hunters had wiped out large numbers of grizzly, black bear, cougar, and wolf populations, predators that were deemed a threat to cattle and sheep. Hydraulic and stream-dredge mining had irreparably altered thousands of miles of water systems. Salmon were declining as the canning industry processed huge amounts of fish along the Pacific Coast. Overgrazing by cattle destroyed thousands of acres of grasslands. Even the once seemingly endless forests of the West were shrinking and overcut.[13]

Americans seemed to have mastered nature in the West, and the miners and railway workers who made up the industrial workforce potentially fit Karl Marx's theories on how industrial life alienated people from their natural world, a process that began when Europeans and Americans moved from an agricultural society to an industrial, urban way of life. Yet a closer look at the lives of Mountain West workers tells a different story.[14] Snowslides occurred in all the major ranges of the Mountain West, and the population growth that came with the proliferation of industrial jobs put more people in contact with environmental hazards. Far from controlling nature, people faced continuous threats.[15] Indeed, those in the extractive and transportation industries fought constantly against environmental challenges. Blizzards loaded the peaks with snow. Steep mountainsides and deep gullies meant that in winter "miners and others working on the slopes of the mountains are obliged to be continually on the lookout" for avalanches.[16]

Thus, workers living in the regions were not alienated from their surroundings but rather were forced to build an understanding of the mountains based on the environmental realities of their work situations. Over time, Mountain West workers accumulated a store of knowledge about their work *and* their natural environment that influenced the decisions they made as they went about the business of living in Avalanche Country. That knowledge would ultimately influence the workplace and rescue efforts within their communities and would lead to challenges to liability law that saw avalanches as acts of God.

The mountains that acted as the physical boundaries of Avalanche Country and the snow that covered its peaks and valleys became actors in the theater of western industrialization. The very substance of the mountains—the animal pelts and the gold and silver found in the streams, soil, and rocks—drew European Americans to the area and then propelled the economic and social transitions that took place there. The height, slope, cold, ice, and snow of the mountains would shape the experiences of Avalanche Country inhabitants—from the trappers who came in the 1820s to the sojourners, miners, and railway workers who followed into the West.

ONE

SURVIVAL STRATEGIES: 1820-1860

These storms have proved fatal to great numbers of trappers and Indians in
and about the Rocky Mountains. They are composed of a violent descent of
snow, hail, and rain, attended with high and piercing wind, and frequently
last three or four days. The storm prevented our seeing the object for which
we were directing our course. We all became saturated with the driving rain
and hail, and our clothing and robes were frozen stiff; still we kept moving,
as we knew it would be certain death to pause on our weary course.

—Jim Beckwourth

T HE FIRST EUROPEAN AMERICANS TO LIVE YEAR-ROUND IN THE
Mountain West were the fur trappers and traders who began to arrive
in the early 1820s. Money and a hope for excitement lured some, like
Warren Angus Ferris, who left the bustling streets of St. Louis in 1830 to
work as a trapper for the American Fur Company. He later wrote in his
memoirs that he went west because of "curiosity, a love of wild adventure,
and perhaps also a hope for profit" and "the strong desire of seeing strange
lands, of beholding nature in the savage grandeur of her primeval state."[1]
What he experienced more than satisfied his hopes. He found the mountains to be of "the most romantic order" and thrilled at the sight of a herd
of bison that he numbered in the thousands: "I never realized before the
majesty and power of the mighty tides of life that heave and surge in all
great gatherings of human or brute creation." He ecstatically proclaimed:
"The scene had here a wild sublimity of aspect, that charmed the eye with
a spell of power, while the natural sympathy of life with life made the pulse
bound and almost madden with excitement. Jove but it was glorious!"[2]
Ferris wrote page after page about the exhilarating landscape, but he was
more than just a sightseer. The grueling work as a trapper dominated his
experiences in what is today Wyoming, Montana, and Idaho, and he suffered hunger, frostbite, sunburn, driving rain, and frigid temperatures.

The risks trappers undertook were formidable, and two out of five who braved this lifestyle would die in the mountains.[3]

The North American fur trade developed first in the Northeast. In Canada in the seventeenth and eighteenth centuries, American Indian trappers and then the offspring of European men and American Indian women, called Métis, did most of the actual trapping. First the French, and then the British, set up trading posts—or factories, as the Hudson's Bay Company called them—along major waterways, where trappers could bring the furs they had accumulated over the season. People traveled by canoe or bateau (a flat-bottomed boat) in the warmer months and by snow-shoe in winter. American Indian women participated in these exchanges by providing essential skills such as sewing moccasins and trapping small game for fur and food. Over time, intermarriage between white trappers and traders and American Indian women became the central economic and diplomatic relationship of Canadian fur trade society.[4]

The Rocky Mountain fur trade arose out of interest by the United States and Great Britain in extending their trapping empires. These ambitions intensified after the War of 1812, as both nations turned their attention to the vast resources of the American West. The well-established British company—the Hudson's Bay Company—came first to trap along the Snake and Missouri Rivers and their tributaries. In 1822, Americans William H. Ashley and Andrew Henry sent trappers from St. Louis to the Rocky Mountains, but the Blackfeet forced their retreat. Ashley and Henry sponsored another party the next year, this time meeting with success. John Jacob Astor's American Fur Company and Ashley and Henry's Rocky Mountain Fur Company soon dominated the region, and by 1830 they controlled fur trading in the Snake River, Green River, and Salt Lake Basins.[5]

Although experiences in other parts of North America influenced the development of the Rocky Mountain fur trade, the western trade took on unique characteristics. The so-called factory system used by the British in the Northeast and the brigade system used by the British and Americans in the Northwest did not work as well in the Rockies because of the difficult terrain, the distance between the mountains and eastern cities, and competition between trapping companies. The Canadian factory system was based on permanent trading posts and relied heavily on white, American Indian, and Métis trappers. The brigade system also used permanent trading posts, but companies involved in this system sent out teams of mostly white trappers into the interior. The Rocky Mountain fur trade evolved from the factory system and the brigade system. The new hybrid system was credited to partners Ashley and Henry, who recognized that trying to compete with the Hudson's Bay Company on the Snake and Missouri Rivers would not be profitable. Instead they would seek the beaver that lived along the smaller mountain streams. Ashley and Henry also saw permanent posts as too difficult and expensive to stock and maintain, especially in the wintertime. Additional problems, such as frequent attacks by the Blackfeet near the Missouri River, affirmed their decision to move south and west into the mountains. Their fur-trading system involved sending groups of trappers on horses into the mountains with the agreement that they would all meet again in early summer.[6] The location of the meeting site changed from year to year. The rendezvous system, as it came to be called, depended on these yearly gatherings in which the fur companies and traders purchased furs from independent trappers and collected the furs their employees or debtors had accumulated since the last meeting. The traders who brought goods to the rendezvous profited by as much as two thousand percent.[7] The furs then went overland and by water, usually to St. Louis and points east, and after the summertime rendezvous the mountain men went back to their work.

The rendezvous system grew to include large outfits of up to fifty men employed by companies, independent trappers who worked for themselves (men Warren Ferris referred to as Free Men, or men who traded with all companies), and skin trappers who worked on credit, borrowing supplies against a predetermined number of skins that they were expected to bring to rendezvous. Employees of the companies, such as cooks, hunters, and guides, along with local Indians descended on the rendezvous site to take advantage of the goods and entertainment: trading, gambling, drinking, and horse races. Moving the summer rendezvous site accommodated the mobile and seasonal nature of the Rocky Mountain fur trade. After the rendezvous, trappers typically worked through the fall, found a place to hole up during the worst of the winter, and resumed their work in the spring.[8]

CHALLENGING TERRAIN

The mountainous terrain meant most of the traveling had to be done on foot or horseback.[9] Trapper Warren Ferris found that such transport meant sometimes trappers could travel only five or six miles a day:

The sides of the mountains were very steep, and were covered with green or fallen pines, of which the latter were so interlocked with each other, and so numerous, that we were continually forced to leap our horses over them, and were frequently compelled to retrace our steps and seek some other passage.[10]

In another location, slide debris frustrated Ferris, and he complained, "Here, an avalanche of huge rocks, trees, and snows had been precipitated from the summit of the mountains, and the sharp fragments left in the route, if slightly disturbed, would immediately resume their headlong course downward, and presented a barrier not only impossible for horses, but even for men."[11] And that was in the summer.

In the winter, the weather and terrain took on a whole new shape. Because the search for beaver extended along both sides of the Rocky Mountains, trappers were exposed to some of the most extreme topography and weather North America had to offer. In a place where "it was said there were only three months—July, August, and Winter"—the trappers found the reality not that different from the jokes.[12] Swollen rivers, bears, and American Indians threatened the men in the summer months, and inclement winter weather tested them the rest of the year. Winter could dominate two-thirds of the calendar and snow could fall at any time at higher elevations. For instance, during a visit to Big Hole, Montana, a summer snowstorm ruined several days of hunting for Ferris, and in September, another storm held him up. Although ideally trappers settled in to winter quarters, safe from snowstorms and freezing temperatures, the nature of their occupation and reliance on game for food put them outside every month of the year.

Survival depended on the trappers' ability to move safely and efficiently through their landscape, their skill for finding food, and their knowledge about the tools of their trade, such as guns, knives, and traps. It also depended on their ability to take care of their horses and one another. Some brought such knowledge with them, but the particular geography and weather of the Rocky Mountains often required adaptation of previously learned skills to new conditions, and many European Americans entered this environment with little experience in living off the land. Ferris confessed that on setting out for the mountains he was "unused to a life so purely aboriginal"; and Osborne Russell, who worked in the Rocky Mountains from 1834 to 1843, proclaimed himself a "raw hand" when he arrived.[13] Although one of his relatives claimed that Russell worked for several years in Wisconsin and Minnesota for the Northwest Fur Trapping and Trading Company before going west, Russell clearly encountered new challenges. His stories of trapping in the mountains confirmed that he learned many of his lessons the hard way, or, as Russell put it, he had "been chiefly educated in Nature's School under that rigid tutor experience."[14]

One hazard came after snowstorms.[15] Russell and a companion thought nothing of the sunlight reflecting off the fresh snow until their unprotected eyes felt "as if they were filled with coarse Sand" for four days.[16] Snow blindness, impaired vision caused by "sunburning" one's eyeballs, represented a previously unknown and potentially dangerous affliction for men who relied on their eyes for survival as they walked or rode through the mountains. Ferris, too, suffered from snow blindness, writing of being "nearly deprived of sight from inflammation of the eyes, brought on by the reflection of the sunbeams on the snow."[17]

The extreme cold also challenged the trappers. When temperatures dropped, Ferris walked and led his horse to keep from freezing, and he treated frostbite by sticking frozen limbs in snow. Trapper James Clyman also walked rather than rode when temperatures dipped. Even the task of procuring water became a terrible chore in extreme temperatures. When streams and rivers froze, men had to either melt snow, "a tedious and vexatious process," or get the water some other way.[18] Clyman recalled in his narrative of Rocky Mountain life how he rescued his group of men and horses from dehydration. While he watched thirstily, his comrades attempted to chop a hole in the ice that blocked access to the stream. When that method failed, Clyman shot his gun into the ice and water gurgled up, providing enough for all.[19]

Trappers' horses suffered in the harsh conditions as well. Russell found that his horse did not flounder in the snow when a frozen crust encased the drifts, so he made it a habit to leave camp early in the morning, before the sun had softened the ice-encrusted snow. Not following this practice could mean horses plunged through, cutting their legs horribly. Even if they did not suffer injuries, horses sank so deeply into sun-softened snow that they made extremely slow progress; already weakened by short rations, they quickly became exhausted. While details are lacking, Ferris wrote that at one point, "there was no alternative but for us to carry them [the horses]. . . . we therefore procured poles, and transported them two miles through the snow to the hillside."[20] The next day, to spare the horses, the men tramped down snow by foot, creating a trail six miles long that led to bare ground. Ferris's relief was obvious:

The sensation produced by this sudden transition from one vast and deep expanse of snow which had continually surrounded us for more than five months, to an open and unencumbered valley of one hundred miles in diameter, over which the sun shed its unclouded warmth, and where the greenness of starting verdure gladdened the eye, was one of the most exquisite and almost rapturous pleasures. Our toils were past, our hardships were over.[21]

When horses flailed, trappers often turned to snowshoes for transportation. Records indicate that Rocky Mountain trappers relied on the racket style of snowshoe introduced to European Americans by the American Indians of the Northeast.[22] The Hudson's Bay Company had hired northeastern Iroquois on their crews, and the Iroquois might have introduced snowshoes to the Americans in the West. Plains Indians also hunted on snowshoes in winter, so western trappers could have borrowed the technique from them. Ferris relied on his snowshoes but found using them tedious: "To chase, on snow shoes, half or three fourths of a day over spurs of mountains, kill a deer and pack it on your back to camp two or three miles, might do as an occasional amusement, but when necessity makes it an everyday business it becomes rather tiresome."[23] Men also used snowshoes to cover long distances. One legendary mountaineer, Thomas Fitzpatrick, went from Utah to Missouri on snowshoes. He left in February with a promise to return with supplies to Cache Valley by the first of July. After a series of adventures almost impossible to believe (from defeating dehydration to surviving an Indian attack), Fitzpatrick was reunited with his fellow mountaineers.[24]

The trappers' mode of living demanded they accrue skills and technologies to lessen the risks they undertook. Their possessions—guns, knives, snowshoes, horses—provide material evidence of this. Yet more than just physical responses, survival techniques led men to recast the way they viewed risk. For instance, Ferris's experiences induced deep thinking that led him to consider what drew men to the mountains and why they stayed. What exactly was the "charm" of this "rude, nomadic, and hazardous mode of life?" he wondered. Why would men "estrange themselves from home, country, friends, and all comforts, elegances and privileges of civilization?" He concluded that the "very danger has its attraction, and the courage and cunning, and skill, and watchfulness made necessary by the difficulties they have to overcome, the privations they are forced to contend with, and the perils against which they must guard, become at once their pride and boast"[25] must be the motivation. But in spite of the "perils" and "privations," it appeared to him that the trappers possessed a happiness not found in the towns and cities in the East, implying that living on the edge of "society" led to a singular satisfaction.

In 1846, another observer thought,

> The trappers of the Rocky Mountains belong to a *genus* more approximating to the primitive savage than perhaps any class of civilized man. Their lives being spent in the remote wilderness of mountains, with no other companion than Nature herself . . . their sole care is to procure sufficient food to support life, and the necessary clothing to protect them from the rigorous climate. . . . Constantly exposed to perils of all kinds, they become callous to any feeling of danger.[26]

Writer Washington Irving called the trappers he encountered in the West "the Mountaineers," bringing together where they lived, their identity, and their work. He believed western trappers and traders represented a "totally different class" of men.[27] His depiction of the mountaineers created an enduring image of the mountain man as "hardy, lithe, vigorous and active; extravagant in word, and thought, and deed; heedless of hardship; daring of anger; prodigal of the present, and thoughtless of the future."[28]

Trapper Russell, however, revealed a more nuanced explanation of risk assessment, explaining that he consciously dealt with risk by delaying his mental processing of the event. He rarely thought of the danger as he scaled icy climbs or crossed dangerous crevices. Only later did his "blood run cold to meditate upon the scenes I had passed thro. During the day and often have I resolved never to risk myself again in such places and as often broken the resolution."[29] In one case, the reward of catching a choice mountain sheep propelled him to risk life and limb, and his mental trick of deferring fear until after the danger had passed allowed him to put meat on his campfire and gave him the energy he needed to go out the next day and engage in the physical work of laying traps and skinning beaver. "The sight of danger," he noted, "is less hideous than the thought of it."[30]

COOPERATION AND CAMPFIRE TALES

The commonsense practices, skills, and risk assessment used by individual trappers proved essential to survival, but more complex cooperative behaviors also became part of their world. The harsh environment contributed to how men interacted with one another, understood responsibility, and evaluated their comrades. Impressions of the mountain men as entirely uncivilized and self-sufficient have held sway in the American imagination, but in truth this description of the trapper bears little resemblance to the real man and fails to acknowledge the reliance they had on others.

Trappers, like many other European Americans on the frontier, benefited from the knowledge they acquired from American Indians. Crafting and using snowshoes were skills passed along from Indians to western trappers, who then passed knowledge along to those who came later. And although inexperienced trappers built log cabins at winter quarters, experience taught veterans that bison skin lodges (tents or teepees), like those constructed by the Indians, made better shelters. Tents stayed warm and cozy even during the coldest days, and the hole at the top let out smoke and let in light. Six or seven men might share such a shelter for months at a time. They spent the hours telling stories, passing books around among those who could read, visiting with anyone camped nearby, and sharing holiday celebrations.Some trappers spent the winter with groups of Indians, using the sedentary months to marry and spend time with their wives, and learning and improving their language skills, all of which facilitated relations between the two groups.[31]

Trapper Russell improved his chances of survival as a result of the experience he acquired over the years. At first he worked for Jim Bridger's Rocky Mountain Fur Company, traveling in groups of up to forty men that included trappers, camp keepers, and cooks. Even after he quit the company, he still almost always traveled with one or more companions, both white trappers and Indians. Skills he acquired as a linguist and negotiator allowed him to trade and camp with the Snake and Nez Percé peoples. He seldom traveled without his "old comrade Elbridge," and explained: "I say old comrade because we had been some time together, but he was a young man . . . he was not much of a landsman, woodsman or hunter, but a great, easy good-natured fellow."[32] In the winter they sought out shelter and companionship at Fort Hall, near present-day Pocatello, Idaho—a site chosen because it was often spared the region's worst weather.[33] When Ferris's horse threw him near Smith's Fork on the Bear River, breaking his gun in the process, he urged his readers to consider how a trapper might feel "after losing his only means of subsistence and defence, in hourly danger of his life and thrown entirely upon the charity of his comrades."[34] If a trapper in such circumstances became separated from his companions, death was almost certain.

Cooperation in the field was essential for staying alive, but the companionship men found working and living together provided needed social outlet, too. Trappers formed friendships and partnerships that eased the homesickness that accompanied mountain living. After months alone in the field, reunion with friends was cause for celebration. As Ferris described these reunions, the trappers "exchanged salutes, and hastened to grasp the honest hands of our hardy old comrades, glad to meet and mingle with them again after a long absence, and listen to their adventures, or recount our own."[35] More than just campfire entertainment, the stories contributed to the collective store of knowledge and sense of identity they shared. According to Ferris, they all "told as extravagant yarns as they pleased, and we believed as little as we liked."[36]

One popular tale was about trapper Hugh Glass. One day in 1822 or 1823, Glass moved ahead of his hunting party, at which point he unexpectedly encountered "a female bear, accompanied by her two cubs." The bear "fell upon him, cast him to the ground, and deliberately commenced devouring him."[37] When the other trappers caught up with Glass, they promptly "destroyed the grizzly monsters."[38] Believing Glass's death imminent, the company commander, Andrew Henry, paid two men to stay behind to bury him once he passed the veil. After five days, however, the "heartless wretches," tired of waiting and afraid of Indians, took Glass's rifle and shot pouch and left him to die. When they caught up with their party they announced that Glass had perished. Imagine their surprise when Glass appeared at a trading post many months later![39] How did he survive?

As one young trapper heard the tale, Glass regained consciousness, found his companions and equipment gone, and dragged himself to a spring where he quenched his thirst. Slowly regaining his strength, he committed himself to "crawling and hobbling" three hundred miles to Fort Kiowa on the Missouri River, "sustaining life with berries and the flesh of a [bison] calf, which he captured from a pack of wolves and devoured raw."[40] After his ordeal, Glass continued on as a trapper until Arikara Indians killed him on the Upper Missouri in 1833.[41]

The tale of Glass's experiences demonstrate the value of endurance and bravery in the mountains—attributes the hero had in spades. It also vilified the "greenhorn" cowards who left Glass to die. Compounding their dastardly deed of abandoning him, they took his gun and powder, the tools most essential for survival. The failure of his companions to stay by his side provided an instructive note about the kind of men future trappers might want to avoid. By telling these sorts of stories trappers began the process of building a rough social space that blended wilderness craft, exchanges of knowledge between American Indians and newcomers, and expectations of behavior from their fellow trappers. Economic motivations drove the interactions between trappers and their environment, but the difficult terrain and harsh weather pushed them to learn from Indians, to become experts on their surroundings, and to cooperate to survive. Like the story of Hugh Glass, the stories trappers told also offer insight into traits they found desirable in their comrades. The risks undertaken by trappers were mitigated by the security they gained from personal expertise or from the help and experience of companions.[42] The accumulation of knowledge during this period of time would inform the experiences of the next wave of settlers to the West, those who made the journey on the Overland Trail to Oregon and California.

FROM TRAPPERS TO GUIDES

Trapping was rarely a lifelong career; most of the men turned to other jobs after fifteen to twenty years of field experience. The Rocky Mountain fur trade itself was short-lived, collapsing by the late 1830s because of dwindling beaver populations as a result of overhunting and a changing fashion market that clamored for silk rather than beaver-felt hats.[43] New opportunities in the West, however, meant that the three thousand veterans of the trade found their skills useful in different occupations. Most stayed in the West, perhaps feeling, as one trapper put it, that he had become "'unfitted to return to former haunts or avocations, with minds alienated by new connections . . . and habits transformed by constant excitement and daring adventure . . . and thrilling aspect of border life, open to the aggression of the savage and the pursuit of free will, free trade and free thinking.'"[44] Former trappers found work in ranching, farming, interpreting, trading, and guiding. Others settled in the communities that had grown up around trading posts.

Some former trappers became legends. Jim Bridger, who reportedly was one of the greenhorns who left Hugh Glass to die, went on to establish himself as a renowned Indian fighter and explorer. Kit Carson, who also got his start as a trapper, went on to work for the U.S. government as a "culture broker," playing a key role in events such as the forced removal by the federal government of the Navajo from their lands.[45] Others toiled more anonymously as guides for European Americans crossing the plains and mountains, bound for Oregon and California.[46]

Trappers made essential contributions to the knowledge that the rest of America gained about the topography and environment of the Mountain West. Albert Gallatin, a politician, Secretary of the Treasury, and advisor to several presidents concerning the United States's territorial boundaries with Great Britain, often referred to the map made by renowned trapper Jedediah Smith for William Ashley. David Burr, geographer for the U.S. House of Representatives, used Smith's map when designing the 1839 "Map of the United States," which was widely used by emigrants, politicians with dreams of empire, and future map makers.[47] Although Ferris's map of the northwest fur country was not published until a century after he drew it, the level of detail he included demonstrates the concrete knowledge that the trappers had of the terrain they crisscrossed.

GUIDES AND GUIDEBOOKS

After the trappers, European American missionaries came to the area, intent on converting Indians. The missionaries began making the trip overland to Oregon Territory in the mid-1830s. The first of these men and women relied on fur traders to guide and protect them as they traveled west. In 1836, the first white women made the overland journey, sending the signal that families could safely make the trip. From 1846 to 1848, the settlement process accelerated. In 1846, the "year of decision," as one historian characterized it, the United States entered a war with Mexico and negotiated the border in the Northwest with Great Britain. At the same time, the Latter-day Saints, known as Mormons, began their exodus from Illinois to Utah.[48] By 1848, the war with Mexico was over and gold had been discovered at Sutter's Fort in California, transforming the trickle of emigrants west into a flood. The population of European Americans in California jumped from 14,000 in 1848 to around 223,000 four years later.[49] At the same time, the populations of Oregon and Utah increased, as did Colorado's after the discovery of gold in Cherry Creek in 1858, near present-day Denver.

The risks Overlanders faced were considerable, but most made the trip westward safely. Unlike the trappers' high mortality rate, these pioneers died at a rate equivalent to those who stayed home: Of the 250,000 who made the trip before 1860, only around 4 percent, or 10,000, died on the trail.[50] Most who died succumbed to diseases like cholera or from "carelessness," such as drowning (as many as 300) or accidental gunshot wounds.[51] Some families turned around before reaching their destination, deciding the rewards at the end of the trail could not possibly be worth the hardships they had encountered to that point.[52]

Before 1850, hired guides and guidebooks remained the most important sources of information about the journey. By the mid-1840s, newspaper articles and pamphlet-style guidebooks offered the most accessible and affordable sources of information. These inexpensive guidebooks gave advice on everything from what to pack to practical suggestions about working with mules and oxen.[53] This information shaped the ideas of what would be encountered along the trail and suggested ways to cope with difficulties. These guidebooks included Lansford W. Hastings's *Emigrants' Guide to Oregon and California* (1845); Edwin Bryant's *What I Saw in California* (1848–1849), printed serially in newspapers in the East; and William Clayton's *The Latter-Day Saints' Emigrants' Guide* (1848).[54]

But even as the journey west became more common, printed information about the trails offered inconsistent and decidedly bad advice. Sometimes the information did not come from firsthand experience. Useless travel tips, hyperbolic descriptions of the landscape, and poorly drawn maps increased the danger of the journey.[55] Hastings personally led a group safely to California, but his guidebook was full of misinformation. The infamous Donner party, who left Illinois for California in 1846, ran into trouble after following the book's advice instead of trapper James Clyman's, who told them to follow the old route.[56] One misfortune followed another. The Donner party found they had to hack a new wagon trail through Weber Canyon in the Wasatch, going only thirty-six miles in twenty-one days.[57] Next, the grueling six-day high desert crossing left both humans and animals thin and exhausted. Weeks passed before the scraggly bunch reached the Sierra Nevada: their last obstacle. Here, one of two men who had been sent ahead for supplies met the weary travelers with seven mules loaded with goods. But the first snows had already fallen and blown into drifts as high as ten feet in the mountains; nevertheless, the group pressed on until fierce storms trapped them at Truckee Lake (now Donner Lake), below the pass. In spite of Hastings's descriptions of the forbidding mountains that could have deterred anyone, the party did not suspect that deciding to wait out the storm would prove their downfall. They obviously had little comprehension of the amount of snow that could fall in early autumn in the mountains of California.

While those caught at the lake faced the grim winter ahead, James Reed, who had been banished from the party after he killed a cotraveler and had gone ahead to Sutter's Fort in the Sacramento Valley, worked tirelessly to get men and supplies to take back over the mountains to the wife, children, and companions he had left behind on the eastern side. On February 18, the first relief party arrived at the lake and rescued twenty-three sufferers. The inability of the rescuers to pack in many provisions, however, meant those left behind turned to shoe leather, their pet dogs, and finally their dead companions for sustenance. Two more relief parties rescued all but five of the party, who were too sick to travel. Finally, in April, a salvage party went to gather the goods left behind at the camp. Only Lewis Keseberg remained alive, surrounded by the half-eaten remains of his comrades.[58] By the end of the winter, the original eighty-seven members of the Donner party had dwindled to forty-seven.[59]

Choosing a bad guide had dire consequences, but even the most knowledgeable and experienced leaders could not always protect emigrants from the harsh environment. Stephen Meek, a former mountain man and experienced guide, led 1,000 emigrants straight into disease and disaster when he took them on the ill-conceived (but aptly named) Malheur River route to Oregon in 1845. Although he had earned his credentials by assisting his brother Joseph in leading the Walker missionary party in 1840, in this instance his directions proved less efficacious and he so incited the rage of the emigrants that he abandoned the group in fear for his life. He went to The Dalles, a community on the Columbia River, where he organized a rescue party.[60] Meek, unlike guidebook writer Hastings, had to deal directly with the results of his mismanagement. But the unfortunates who followed him had to contend with hunger, exhaustion, and death just the same, and as many as seventy-five perished.[61]

In Utah, Latter-day Saints tried to ease the journey for new emigrants by organizing their trip from beginning to end, providing experienced guides, and sending relief parties from Salt Lake City with food and wagon teams. Even with this assistance, decisions to leave too late in the season could lead to disaster. In 1856, two parties of Saints pulling handcarts encountered trouble with early winter storms in Wyoming. Of the 1,076 who left Iowa City, more than 200 died before rescuers arrived and led them to Salt Lake.[62] The centralized organization of the Latter-day Saints made their experiences different from those of the Donner and Meek parties, yet the basic lessons learned about making the trip successfully were the same: Use a good guide or guidebook, bring enough supplies, and by all means do not get caught in the mountains in winter.[63]

Although travelers did not have identical experiences, they connected with their environment when they forded streams or struggled through snowdrifts. But beyond physical connections, the trip often pushed them to combine their experiences and knowledge to fit the situation. Joining resources and cooperative behavior were tenets of Mormonism, but the Meek and Donner rescues suggested that disasters encouraged people to act cooperatively in similar ways. The need to learn new skills, rely on those with more experience, and cope with disasters spoke to the precarious nature of this dynamic period, and the survival strategies used led to the emergence of a distinctive social space that mixed meeting the wilderness challenges of the West with the practices and institutions brought from elsewhere. Their newfound knowledge would become even more important when European Americans sought to live permanently at increasingly remote locations at high elevations.

TWO

MOUNTAIN MINERS, SKIING MAILMEN, AND ITINERANT PREACHERS: 1850-1895

A horse in order to be of any use in carrying the mail over the mountain
ridges must, like his driver, be an expert snow-shoer.

—H. G. Squier (1891)

The killing of Pat McEnany by a snowslide takes away another old pioneer,
one who spent the best years of his life in the mountains seeking the shining
metal. . . . It was found that his neck and back were both broken, and the only
consolation his friends have is, that he did not know what killed him.

—*The San Juan* (1887)

THE DISCOVERY OF GOLD AT SUTTER'S FORT IN CALIFORNIA IN
1848 changed everything in the West. The population of European
Americans in California jumped from 14,000 in 1848 to 223,000 four
years later.[1] The discovery of gold in Cherry Creek near present-day Denver, Colorado, in 1858, ignited a similar rush to the Rocky Mountains of
Colorado. And after the 1859 Pikes Peak rush, other parts of Colorado
aroused interest in potential emigrants. Early explorations into the San
Juan Mountains, particularly two expeditions led by Charles Baker in 1860
and 1861, indicated rich gold and silver deposits lay buried there. In the
1860s, the area that prospectors generally referred to as the San Juan Country encompassed most of the southwestern portion of Colorado Territory.[2]
Violent clashes between the white settlers and the Ute Indians, however,
discouraged prospectors from going to this area until the U.S. government
yielded to pressure from the mining community and ceded all the mineral
rights to prospectors under the 1873 Brunot Agreement. Conflicts between
the miners and the Utes continued for the next few years, and eventually led to the U.S. Army's systematic removal of the Utes to reservations

on less profitable land.[3] Subsequent mineral strikes, or the hopes of them, drove people higher into the mountains. Some of Colorado's most productive mines, such as Leadville, sat well above 9,000 feet. The first winter in the San Juans found "fully two thousand prospectors ... at work, and before midsummer it" was estimated that at least ten thousand more would "endeavor to woo the giddy goddess."[4] In the next ten years the Colorado towns of Silverton, Ouray, Lake City, and Rico would develop and become connected by roads, trails, and rails. Avalanches occurred frequently, and the miners who went into these mountains beginning in the 1870s found themselves confronting a particularly dangerous environment.

Similar to southwestern Colorado, Alta, Utah, the primary settlement in the Little Cottonwood Canyon, boomed with the detection of silver in the 1860s.[5] Before 1858, Latter-day Saints who settled near the Great Salt Lake used Little Cottonwood Canyon's granite, timber, and water. The first real population increase in Little Cottonwood Canyon began in the early 1870s, when Alta's population climbed from 216 in 1870 to 8,000 in 1872, after the discovery of silver. The opening of Little Cottonwood Canyon was about ten miles southeast of Salt Lake City and climbed steeply from roughly 4,200 feet at its mouth to 9,700 feet at its terminus in the Wasatch Mountains.[6] The canyon walls and heavy snows created perfect avalanche conditions.[7] Slides happened repeatedly in the region, often with deadly force. During the winter of 1874 alone, the *Salt Lake Daily Tribune* reported four harmless slides, one deadly slide, one that carried a man 4,000 feet but deposited him safely, and one that nearly obliterated the stage line.[8]

Prospectors then, like the trappers who traversed the mountains before them, found themselves updating winter survival strategies or acquiring skills not needed before their move to the mountains. For instance, like the trappers before them, prospectors adopted methods of preventing snow blindness, adjusting their actions to fit particular hazards in the Mountain West. Dr. Charles Fox Gardiner, who worked in and around Aspen, Colorado, in the second half of the nineteenth century, explained that greenhorns, who failed to protect their eyes, "were often attacked. Showing first by a redness of the lids and a profuse flow of tears."[9] The symptoms then "rapidly developed into a fearful, stabbing pain of the eyeballs, loss of sight; and in severe cases the patient became crazy for a time, running about and dashing into everything in his way."[10] As a precaution people who had to travel during the daytime would blacken their faces, "taking some burnt wood from a stump" to minimize the shine off their faces or dressed in dark clothes to reduce reflection and the risk of snow blindness.[11] Others wore veils to shield their eyes.[12]

Knowing how to prevent snow blindness had obvious advantages, but learning when to travel also proved an essential accommodation during the prospecting era. As seen with trappers, the harsh environment had an impact on people's relationships with their horses and pack animals. The dramatic swing in temperatures caused by sunny days in the western mountains made the slopes susceptible to snowslides and also affected surface snow in flatter places. For those without mountain know-how, problems could begin when a newcomer tried to travel in soft snow and his pack animal fell up to its hocks in the drifts. According to one account in *Harper's Weekly,* burros, also called donkeys, balked when caught in the snow, and prospectors spent a fair amount of time shoveling out their animals and cajoling them along the trail.[13] Rev. John L. Dyer, a minister for the Colorado Conference of the Methodist Episcopal Church, discovered that the winter sun could soften the snow so much that it could not "bear a man in the daytime, even with snow-shoes. From about two o'clock in the morning until nine or ten in the morning was the only time a man could go; and a horse could not go at all."[14] For men like Dyer, whose job required mobility, being able to travel in winter was a requirement and necessitated familiarity with the climate and landscape.

Storms could blow up suddenly in Avalanche Country, and snow could obliterate trails or make them exceedingly dangerous. Residents cut blaze marks on trees alongside the trails that could be followed even when deep snow fell, in the hopes of sparing travelers from getting lost.[15] But even staying on a trail did not protect people and animals from dangerous situations. Ice underneath the snow might cause a man to slip and fall to his death over the edge of a cliff. One preventive technique called "tailing" put the burden of safety on the donkey. The miner "takes his burro by the tail . . . and hangs on like grim death, carefully feeling his way along to the bottom or over the worst part."[16] In another case, a prospector, caught in a snowstorm, claimed three burros dug him out of the snow and led him to safety. He declared, "Yes, I have a warm place in my heart for these little animals—yes, I may call it reverence."[17] People therefore not only depended on their pack animals to carry their bodies and their supplies to remote claims; they also found themselves working closely with their sure-footed companions on steep descents and trusting them to navigate through tricky situations.

Preventing snow blindness, knowing when to travel, and learning to work with pack animals was crucial, but knowing the appropriate mode of travel was perhaps most important. Before roads and rails came to the mountains, skis were the most common and vital tool for winter travel.[18] In the Sierra Nevada after the California gold rush and for trappers and miners in the Rocky Mountains, skiing became elemental to working and traveling in winter. Norwegian immigrants first brought skiing to America, and those who used the seven- to twelve-foot wooden skis sometimes called them Norwegian snowshoes, to differentiate them from the racket style of snowshoe used by Indians and trappers. Sources before 1900 refer to what we know as "skis" as "Norwegian snowshoes," "snow-shoes," or "skees." The term "skees" became more common after about 1900, and evolved into "ski." James K. Hastings, who lived in Colorado in the early 1870s, remembered that everyone used "the Norwegian ski. I never saw a man on a French Canadian snowshoe or racket."[19] Reportedly, John A. "Snowshoe" Thompson introduced skiing to California miners in 1856. As a boy in Norway he had grown up around skis, and based on that memory (he had emigrated when 10) he built a pair. He made the skis from green oak: "They were ten feet in length, were four inches in width behind the part on which the feet rest, and in front were four inches and a quarter wide . . . he put them upon a pair of scales, and found that they weighed twenty-five pounds."[20] They were cumbersome, to say the least, and over time mountain people refined their ski-building techniques. Dr. Gardiner was amazed when he first arrived in the mountains and saw everyone whizzing around on their boards. He remarked that

deep snow made it impossible to clear the roads or trails and, very early in the history of these camps, the long, narrow snowshoe, the Norwegian ski, was introduced. Nothing surprised me more in my first sight of this strange settlement than to see people going about on skis. Everyone used them quite as a matter of course, and slid over the top of the deep snow with the utmost skill. Even little children just able to walk were flying about on their little snowshoes.[21]

One observer noted that in the hurry to get to the San Juans, "the greater part of the prospecting in this section was accomplished on snow-shoes [skies]," as hopefuls rushed there in the winter, anxious to begin looking for silver.[22] The Reverend James Joseph Gibbons, one of Colorado's itinerant preachers, stressed that for many parts of the state "where the snow is four feet and upward in depth, all winter long . . . snowshoes are one of the necessaries of life."[23] Prospectors could fashion skis with materials at hand, and when "held up by a heavy snowfall, lacking time and material to improvise snowshoes of Indian pattern, [a man] can always split out and hew a serviceable pair of skees."[24] Singular to the Rockies and other "mountainous regions the skee form of snowshoe is . . . used," as opposed to other regions where "the Indian form of shoe [racket-style] is almost exclusively used."[25] One advantage to long wooden skis was that little skill was required in making them, although some practice was required to master their use; another advantage was that they transported the wearer swiftly downhill. Mountain people relied on their skis to get into town and return with supplies to their camps, and without these pieces of equipment they could not have left their cabins.

For three miners in southwestern Colorado, a combination of newly acquired ski skills and daring escape meant they avoided certain starvation. One day, while working in their tunnel, the men heard the unmistakable roaring sound that meant only one thing: avalanche! They ran to the mouth of the mineshaft to look out and found that their cabin had been swept away, along with all their wood and food stores. The snowslide left the miners facing serious privation if they did not make the trek from their claim, located above tree line, to the town of Needleton several miles away.[26] Deep snow made travel difficult, but these miners had stashed their skis at the opening of their mine, affording them a precarious yet possible way to get down the mountain.

Steep slopes and deep canyons proved a challenge to the miners who "were not experts with the skees. . . . They could manage them fairly well and had used them often 'in the day's work' as men must who go about in the Rocky Mountain country in winter, but in a coast like this they were only amateurs."[27] When forced to jump off a fifty-foot cliff, the first miner landed headfirst in thirty feet of soft snow. Uninjured, he watched the second miner take the plunge successfully. The third man lost his skis midflight and completed two somersaults in the air before landing so deep in the drifts that his friends had to dig him out. They found only one of his skis, and the threesome barely made it into Needleton by nightfall.[28] It was a close call, but the prospectors' combination of new skills and cooperation meant they survived their encounter with an avalanche. Through this near-disaster, the miners gained a greater familiarity with their environment and gained confidence in their ability to deal with catastrophes.

The constant threat of avalanches and the volume of snow in the Mountain West created travel problems for miners and also made supply and communication networks difficult to establish and maintain. The extended winter season in this region made already remote places even more isolated during the cold months. In the prospecting and early hard-rock mining period, mailmen and itinerant preachers emerged as important figures who linked mining camps to one another and to the outside world. The risks undertaken by these year-round travelers and the techniques they acquired for travel contributed to the growing sense of community in the mountains.[29]

Undoubtedly, those who lived in the mountains looked forward to the arrival of the postal carriers, who were often the mountain dwellers' only connection to news about what was happening nearby and afar. Word of mineral strikes as well as labor strikes by men for better pay; accidents; miners' deaths; and other affairs as well as news from loved ones broke the monotony of the long winter months. Mail service allowed mountain residents to communicate with those outside their immediate community without making hazardous trips themselves. Rather, the risk to carry the communication fell on the shoulders of the mail carriers, who themselves had to learn survival techniques in the unforgiving mountains.

California was the first place where deep snows in the mountains pushed the limits of creative mail delivery. Historians give "Snowshoe" Thompson credit not only for introducing skiing to California miners but for also becoming the first mail carrier to use skis to bring the mail over the mountains in the winter. After hearing of the problems others had experienced in getting the mail through when the snow lay deep, Thompson built his first pair of skis and applied for a job as mail carrier. He began carrying the mail between Placerville, California, and Genoa in the Carson Valley in January 1856, making the ninety-mile trip east in three days and the return trip in two. His usual load of mail, which he carried in a backpack, weighed between sixty and eighty pounds. According to Dan De Quille, a journalist who interviewed Thompson in 1876, Thompson did not have the advantage of later inventions like "dope," a "preparation of pitch, tallow, and other ingredients, which being applied to the bottom of the shoes [skis], enables the wearer to lightly glide over snow softened by rays of the sun."[30] In lieu of such modern techniques, Thompson learned that if he traveled "at night, when a crust was frozen on the snow," he avoided clumps of snow sticking to his skis.[31] He believed that if a man paid attention to the terrain, boulders, and trees he would stay on track in the Sierras, and consequently Thompson had little sympathy for people who got lost because they "knew nothing about the course of the prevailing winds, about trees and rocks, or about the stars in the heavens, not to speak of the formation and configuration of the mountains."[32] Thompson turned out to be more than just a mailman; he used his skills to help rescue a man he encountered who had both frostbitten feet and ankles. Thompson skied to Genoa, where he organized a relief party to return to the mountains to fetch the injured man. He then had to ski back to Placerville to get chloroform, because the doctor in Carson Valley determined the victim's ruined limbs had to be amputated but would not perform the surgery without the anesthesia.

Skiing mailmen became fairly common in the late nineteenth century in the Mountain West, with as many as fifty working in Colorado before 1900. Usually under a bidding system, men contracted to carry the mail over particular routes, with a four-year commitment. The contractor would frequently subcontract parts of the route in the winter to men eager to find employment during the mines' less active winter months, and each mailman was responsible for supplying his own equipment.[33] In Colorado, mail carriers attempted to provide regular service, but much depended on the weather. James Hastings, who lived in the Rockies during the winter of 1871–72, when he was a little boy, remembered that as soon as the mailman came into view high on the mountainside above town everyone would gather at the boarding house to watch his progress. Hastings recounted that once, the mailman took a bad fall, breaking a ski, and causing much amusement among the crowd. Of course, Hastings pointed out, the witnesses knew well "that it might have cost his life had it happened an hour earlier and out of sight of the camp."[34] Hastings and others recognized the risks the mailman undertook every time he brought their mail.

Not all carriers fared as well as Hastings's man. Many in the San Juans reminisced about a skiing mail carrier who had disappeared the week before Christmas, his bag full of letters and presents from the East. Some speculated that the carrier had decided to ski off with the valuables. Three years later, however, locals discovered what had really happened: "They found the honest fellow on the farther side of a lake in the shade of a hill frozen in snow and ice, as faithful to his trust, with the mail bag still strapped to his back." He had died in an avalanche.[35]

The uncertainty of the mail's arrival made this connection to "outside," as Steamboat Springs, Colorado, resident Lulie M. Crawford called it, especially important. It intensified residents' sense of isolation from other areas, but it also pulled them together because they shared that tenuous connection with the members of their community. Lulie's journal of her girlhood in the Yampa Valley in the early 1880s noted every time the carrier arrived safely and on time, as well as when he was late and the worry it caused. She wrote on New Year's Day 1881: "Dave [the mailman] came in with the mail. He brought bad news. One of the mail carriers is lost and hasn't been seen or heard of since last Tuesday. Was lost in that dreadful hard storm. Poor fellow!"[36] She also rejoiced when the lost man reappeared, writing, "Good news, yes, just splendid. The mail carrier is found."[37] The weather and the plight of the mailmen shaped Lulie's childhood record.

The persistent interest in the lost mailman near Steamboat led another skiing mailman to tell the story again years later for the Grand Junction newspaper, the *Daily Sentinel*. William T. Snook carried the mail during the winter of 1881 between Steamboat Springs, Rock Creek, and Laramie, Wyoming. He had somewhat less sympathy for the lost man, "who he offered to accompany on his first route but who said " 'no.' " When Coburn, the newcomer, failed to appear on time, Snook began to organize a search party. Remarkably, as noted, Coburn found his way back to his route, where he was found by the search party, but he suffered badly from frostbite. As often occurred in remote places, the locals provided the doctoring until a professional could arrive. Snook explained that he "cut off his [Coburn's] boots with a jackknife. I put his feet in snow and ice, covering him with a blanket. It hurt terribly, of course, but the doctor said it was the best thing I could have done." After awhile the "flesh dropped off the soles of his feet, and wherever the points of his toes rotted, I cut them off. I covered his legs and feet with syrup and flour, and the doctor said that was a good thing too."[38] They expected Coburn to recover, minus a few toes.

Even as the skiing mailmen chanced their lives, they often found the monetary reward less than satisfying. "Snowshoe" Thompson carried the mail across the mountains for twenty years without compensation from the U.S. government, believing that it would pay him even though he never officially signed a contract with the U.S. Postal Service. He finally decided to press for payment, and petitioned Congress for $6,000 for his services. He even went to Washington, D.C. (walking nearly one hundred miles when his train got trapped in snow drifts en route), to claim his due. He ran out of money and had to go home before his hearing, however, and never received compensation. Zene B. Maudlin, another Steamboat mailman, recalled well the trials of his employment and the meagerness of the reward. He had gone to the Yampa Valley to run cattle, but for several winters he took on the work of carrying the mail on skis. He remembered, "I've bucked the wind with 60 or 70 pounds of mail on my back when the thermometer was 35 degrees below zero. What do you suppose Uncle Sam paid me? Forty dollars a month and I boarded myself."[39] Mailmen did not do the job to get rich, but it did provide work in the winter months when ranching and farming duties slowed. It also provided alternative employment for former miners who had decided they preferred not to eke out a living as prospectors or take the risks inherent in hard-rock mining. The mailmen had more control over their bodies, because their safety largely depended on their expertise on skis, and they enjoyed the hospitality and gratitude of isolated communities.

In Plumas, California, the harsh environment meant it was necessary for creatures other than men to learn how to use winter equipment. As some routes became more established, horse-drawn sleighs replaced skiing mailmen. The horses that pulled the mail sleighs wore specially adapted snowshoes that consisted of "large plates of iron or steel some eight or ten inches square, and one fourth of an inch in thickness."[40] The safety of the horse and driver depended on the "intelligence and experience of one of these animals."[41] Horses that learned to use the snowshoes held high value, like "Snow-Shoe Sally," who was well known throughout the district for her ability with the contraptions on her feet.[42]

Other measures that helped keep the mailmen coming year-round included "parties of volunteers" who beat down the trail from their camp. To mark the trail, "At each turn, where a tree may be conveniently situated, they nail a piece of board or shingle in order to indicate the exact location of the road."[43] The efforts made to ensure mail delivery spoke to the importance of contact with other places and illustrated that, even though the climate posed considerable challenges, residents undertook extreme efforts to live as normally as possible.

Itinerant priests and preachers provided another important link between mining camps. In their peregrinations, the preachers made miners at smaller camps feel connected to one another and the outside towns. In addition to providing spiritual healing, performing last rites, and bringing news, priests and preachers brought people together for services. It was not unusual for Protestants and Catholics to worship side by side in these remote mountain communities.[44] In the process of establishing these connections among their parishioners, the clergymen, like the mailmen, learned of the dangers of Avalanche Country and practiced techniques required for traveling and surviving in winter.

Like the lone mailmen, preachers took chances to tend to their flocks, and their ability to survive rested almost entirely on their own abilities. The Reverend John Dyer published an autobiography in which he identified himself as the "snow-shoe itinerant," and explained many of the astounding realities he encountered in Colorado's mountains. Dyer came to Colorado in 1861 from the Midwest, where he had spent time as a farmer, lead miner, and preacher.[45] His first impression of the mountains came in summer, where he found it "different than what I supposed—timber, grass, shrubs of many kinds, strawberry vines in full bloom. . . . I indulged in reflections on the wonders of the creation of God . . . a very Eden Park." His description of such a paradisiacal place suggests that he had anticipated the mountains to be more forbidding. He soon discovered, however, that the winters more than fulfilled his expectations.[46]

Preachers, like other mountain residents, learned to make their own skis, as they were not something easily bought in the nineteenth century. The rapid dissemination of knowledge about skis can partly be attributed to the fact that Norwegians composed a significant portion of the population in the Mountain West. In Alta, for instance, Norwegian immigrants made up one twelfth of the population. In addition to the store of knowledge offered by Norwegian immigrants about skiing, the highly mobile populations of the mining districts, where men traveled great distances to find jobs, exchanged information about winter travel and about the use of skis and other equipment.[47]

A pointed example of the importance of skiing skills came from Dyer, who, like many other residents, had to learn to schuss while in Colorado. Dyer wrote of the process of shaping skis, learning to use them, and the dangers of traveling alone. He recalled that his "snow-shoes were of the Norway style, from nine to eleven feet in length, and ran well when the snow was just right, but very heavy when they gathered snow."[48] He used a single pole to knock off snow that stuck to his skis, and as a rudder when he was going downhill, showing some evolution in the techniques used. He remembered, "On one occasion, as I was going down the mountain . . . my shoes got crossed in front as I was going very fast." He became afraid when he saw "a little pinetree was right in my course, and I could not turn, and dare not encounter the tree with the shoes crossed; and so threw myself into the snow, and went in out of sight."[49] He became more adept on his skis after that, and as a result became the first minister to reach many of the remote mining camps. Dyer also parlayed his newfound skill into a way to supplement his income by carrying mail and other packages in the winter.

COOPERATION

Individual skills mattered, but miners' cooperative use of those skills reduced risk as well. Many prospectors learned the value of cooperative behavior before they even arrived in the gold and silver mines. As in California, many of those who went to Colorado formed "companies" with friends, neighbors, or relatives to pool their resources and make the strenuous trip. On arrival, they acted as partners, buying and working claims together.[50] For example, when H. J. Hawley left Argyle, Wisconsin, for the goldfields of Colorado in 1860, he arrived with six friends and relatives from his hometown. His uncle, Lewis Sargent, a veteran of the California mines, led the company. Visions of instant wealth danced in their heads, and their spirits were buoyed when they bumped into several other companies from Argyle along the way. In Colorado, the men bought a claim together. Hawley and the others benefited from his uncle's experience in California, and cooperative migrations had similar obvious economic advantages when starting out in the mines.

Working with family and friends and forming new connections eased many of the challenges miners confronted, too. For those who came from eastern villages and cities, remembering home and seeking companionship worked as antidotes for the disorienting feelings they often felt when they arrived in mining camps. When Hawley and his Uncle Sargent took a tour around the Colorado mining camps, they learned that prospectors often named their claims after home places: Missouri Flats, Illinois Gulch, Leavenworth Gulch, Virginia Gulch, and Chicago Gulch. These names both signified a longing for homes left behind and identified for others passing through the area the region of the country from which the miners came. Missing home was a common enough feeling, as Hawley lamented at one point, "Give me the old home instead of being in water ankle deep in the Rocky Mountains."[51] Nevertheless, he enjoyed the comradeship he found not just among the men from Wisconsin but also among the men from all over the country who were part of creating the new community. These friendships helped fend off the reality that many of the prospectors felt "rather '*blue*.'"[52] They shared physical and financial hardships, and friendships helped them to manage the mental and physical challenges imposed by mountain living.

Above all, the bonds formed among mountain miners reflected the high value put on friendships in the camps, especially when disaster struck. Although mountain miners did their best to build their homes in places they understood as safe places, showing they had a grasp of the nature of slides, not all slides followed predictable patterns.[53] Sometimes memories of special friendships were all that was left after miners died in slides. In Colorado in 1880, a wall of snow swept over a cabin, smothering the two men inside. Harriet L. Wason, a resident of the San Juans, commemorated their deaths a few years later in a poem, "The Slide at the Empire Mine":

All day a steady snow had drifted down,
Hiding the restful hues of dun and brown
On friendly hill-side, and the slender trail,
That bound us world-ward. Did no spirit quail
At the appalling doom looming before us,
With the unsettled snow-mass trembling o'er us?

If any feared, none spoke; the laugh and jest
Rang out as clear, perhaps with added zest
And but that they who worked at night-shift stood
With outstretched palms, in half unwilling mood
To leave the fire, no outward sign betrayed
If any felt discouraged or dismayed.

The storm had lulled, but the insatiate wind
Trailed a pathetic, vengeful wail behind,

When the brave four took courage, shut the light
And genial glow out from the prying night.

Six yet remained, not one essayed to speak;
The silence broken by a stifled shriek
That blanched all lips, and every man upsprung;
Wide to the night the cabin door was flung.

A rude gust quenched our lamp, and darkness gave
To unknown ill the horror of the grave,
A whirring din, a roll like distant thunder,
On coming, as the hills were rent asunder,
And with hushed breath we each other eyed,
Knowing we faced that awful thing, a slide!

Our world-ward trail was sheltered by a ledge,
(Rising on one side like a rocky hedge,)
That served for shielding some of the cabin door,
And as a quaking mass went thundering o'er
Beyond the trail, leaving it bare and steep,
Into a yawning chasm fathoms deep,
Our unbound hearts leaped upward with a sigh—
For us the King of Terrors had passed by.

The shaft-house from the cabin lay some feet,
Barely five score: but every tempest beat
With cruel fury thro' a small ravine
Across the trail, wholly devoid of screen;
And quite lost now. Instinct our only guide,
We labored blindly and on either side
A comrade found. These both alive were saved,
The shaft-house walls were whole, the roof had caved
And buried two, quite dead, tho' barely cold—
A sight that cowed the bravest to behold.

Will Clark was but a lad, not yet eighteen;
We knew some household darling he had been;
For he had gentle speech and dainty ways,
Appeared to yearn for our good will and praise,
The other, Jack Monroe, was the reverse;

He sandwiched every sentence with a curse,
Defiant seemed, alike of God and man,
To such extremes his daily actions ran;
Yet strange to say, his friendship for the youth
Was strong as death, and beautiful as truth.

We found his giant body wedged between
The splintered rafters; an effectual screen
From their sharp spears, shielding the tender frame
As oft his tongue had sheltered him from blame;
One great hand held the slender fingers close,
One crouched the head in its last long repose,
And thus they sleep, our pitying hands provided,
Who living, loved, in death were not divided.[54]

The possible sexual nature of the friendship between Will Clark and Jack Monroe will remain lost to us (although the poem seems to hint there was one), but what did not disappear was the obvious grief felt by their neighbors, who chose to bury them together. Avalanche tragedies like the one described in this poem highlighted the precarious nature of life and the importance of friendships. The isolation of the camps in winter and the threat of slides—the environmental realities of living in the Mountain West—therefore impressed on many of the miners the importance of the bonds they created with each other.

Miners formed strong friendships, but they made other adaptations, too. One of the reciprocal actions taken by mountain miners that benefited newcomers and old-timers alike came about due to the high probability of travelers getting caught out in snowstorms. As prospectors set up more permanent camps, a "gentlemen's agreement" emerged that held that even when away, they should keep their cabins stocked with wood and food so that if a blizzard blew up any passerby could take shelter.[55] More than simple generosity, this agreement worked mutually, ensuring that all travelers could count on lodging and sustenance. The suddenness and severity of storms influenced customs and led to an honor system that helped people survive.

Encounters with the terrain and climate also led residents to reconsider how to build their houses and to invent methods for finding houses buried under snowdrifts. Practices shared by the camps included building houses with steep, gabled roofs that sloughed off the snow. And where the snow could accumulate up to thirty feet, residents dug tunnels down to their doorways "leading down into the ground like the burrow of a gigantic owl."[56] When snow covered houses, it also became necessary "in some instances, to splice their chimneys in order to get them above the level of the snow."[57] Houses had to be lit day and night because snow covered the windows, and miners also attached "a rag or a tag" to their chimney so they could identify their buried homes when returning from work.[58]

The daily challenges of mountain life, the shared experiences of waiting for mailmen, attending religious services, exchanging gossip, witnessing slides, and crafting skis all contributed to the store of local knowledge. The destructive power of snowslides especially served as a reminder that life in Avalanche Country came with risks. Father Gibbons, who traveled widely in the San Juans as part of his calling, found it "not uncommon to be summoned night or day to sick calls, involving trips of 150 miles."[59] He saw many terrible sights, such as Camp Chattanooga—high in the mountains—destroyed by avalanches. Debris from the houses wrecked by the slide could be found "strewn for half a mile over the valley."[60] He also described places like the Humboldt mine, located at 13,000 feet, where "no trees or sheltering gulches break the force of the awful blizzards which sweep along those naked heights. To witness a snowslide within a short distance of the miner's bunkhouse is no rare occurrence."[61] Ultimately, fear of avalanches did not keep miners and investors away from the mountains, even though abandoned camps destroyed by slides littered the landscape.[62]

Hardships shared across the Mountain West, like environmental problems incident to many regions, contributed to the fabric of life. These adaptations were put to the test as industrial mining overtook camp after camp, and thousands of newcomers faced deep snows and avalanches for the first time. In weighing the risks of dangerous work against the rewards of a wage, the predictability of avalanches would become an important factor as more men and women encountered the hazards of Avalanche Country.

THREE

INDUSTRIAL MINING AND RISK

> The only drawback to the San Juan region is its excessive snow-fall and
> consequent loss of life and property from the deadly avalanche . . . of course
> there is no absolute safeguard against floods, avalanches and cyclones, but
> the Lord provides us with intelligence and expects us to use it. . . . Protection
> may be had against the snow that lays heavy on the hills.
> —*Silverton Standard* (April 14, 1906)

THE GOLD AND SILVER STRIKES THAT PROPELLED PROSPECTORS
westward also attracted corporate investors who had the capital and
technical capabilities to extract the minerals from underground. Of
the 75,000 hopefuls who rushed to Colorado after the 1859 strike, most
found their expectations of striking it rich dashed. Some turned to other
occupations, others went home, but many went to work for the growing
number of corporate-owned mines. By the early 1860s placer and surface mining began to give way to hard-rock underground mining. New
technology that included dynamite (invented in Europe in 1866), power
hoists, pumps, machine drills, and electricity all facilitated the growth of
hard-rock mining in the mountains.[1] Gold and silver mining towns grew
as underground mining techniques improved, and workers came from all
over for jobs in the mines.

Railroads, vital to large-scale mining, replaced the wagon roads in
importance in bringing supplies to and carrying riches out of the camps.
The building of spur lines to mountain communities signaled an important transition in the networks of communication and travel available to
the people who lived and worked there, too. The railways also allowed for
large-scale development. For example, the arrival of the Denver and Rio
Grande line from Durango to Silverton in 1882 brought outside investors, corporate-run mines, underground mining, and men and women
to do the work in the San Juans. Between 1880 and 1890, the populations
of Ouray and San Juan Counties grew from 3,756 to 8,082, an increase

of 215 percent.[2] Newcomers became part of the network of knowledge exchange when those with experience passed on their skills and understanding about how to reduce risk in Avalanche Country.[3]

The arrival of corporate mining and railways significantly increased the number of people in harm's way. Trains that could carry large quantities of ore could also bring supplies year-round to the mountains—and this meant mining companies could hire more people and keep production going throughout the winter. Both the railway employees and the miners who worked in the mountains found themselves confronting more than the usual dangers of their jobs; they also had to contend with the deep snows, freezing temperatures, and avalanches. Not surprisingly, the number of people killed by avalanches increased as the year-round population of the Mountain West grew. Between 1882 and 1893 in San Juan County, avalanches killed twenty-one people, injured four, buried thirty-five who survived, and damaged at least forty different buildings, including seven bunkhouses. This proved a dramatic comparison to the fifteen dead men and ten injured by avalanches between 1875 and 1882.[4] In Alta and the surrounding mine districts, the prerailroad years from 1860 to 1874 saw the death of twenty people by slides. In the decade after the railroad's completion, from 1875 to 1885, snowslides killed at least eighty-six people![5]

As the death toll rose, so did the profits. Between 1882 and 1918, the mines of Silverton alone produced more than $65 million worth of silver.[6] In Utah, between 1870 and 1883, silver mines yielded nearly $46 million.[7] As the mine owners raked in the profits, those who worked in the region throughout the winter found themselves directly in the paths of avalanches. Although slides sometimes interrupted production, the economic imperatives of the corporations pushed managers to operate as continuously as possible.

Aerial tramways that could carry men, supplies, and ore turned into one of the most important devices used in the mountains. Instead of trying to build roads over difficult terrain, tramways' primary function was to carry ore to smelting sites or railroads; they also carried men and materials across gullies, streams, rocky terrain, and snowdrifts. Various tower, cable, and pulley systems were used. Although tramways were not unique to the Mountain West, certain adjustments to their maintenance and construction became essential in Avalanche Country. At the Sunnyside Mine in Colorado, the "company eventually built a fifty-foot tunnel into the mountain to store an emergency spare tower. When a snowslide carried a tower away," the pre-made tower ensured that operations did not have to wait for construction of a new one. At Camp Bird, rather than erecting the tramway in a straight line, "a special angle station to avoid snowslides" was built and "enabled the line to remain open during the winter."[8] Still, the best constructions could not spare men from death and tramways from damage by slides.

The destruction of buildings and accidents that slowed work, or stopped it completely, led to innovations that sought better protection for company property. Tramways sometimes used "extra-heavy timbers or steel supports."[9] Managers in Alta might shut down their mines temporarily in winter when slides seemed likely, thereby offering some protection to their workers. But more often managers decided that profits outweighed safety concerns and would wait to shut operations until after a slide occurred. They depended on structural improvements to keep operations open year-round and reduce risk from slide damage. Some operations built avalanche defense structures, which consisted of log, rock, or earthen wedge-shaped barriers that were meant to deflect snow around a mine shaft, tram tower, or other structure. The efficacy of these defenses proves difficult to determine, but the damage caused by avalanches despite their use suggests they provided little protection.[10]

In addition to the natural risk of avalanches in the region, new mining techniques that used explosives sometimes triggered avalanches. In turn, the accidents with dynamite that caused avalanches to sweep down on the mines led to new ideas about intentionally starting slides before deadly amounts of snow accumulated. Using detonations, however, never became anything more than experimental and sporadic during this period; dynamite and artillery would not come into common usage in the control of avalanches until the middle of the twentieth century.[11] Instead, mine operators followed the most common strategy in dealing with avalanches: prediction and avoidance. By the early 1880s mountain residents recognized that slides often followed the same paths year after year. In addition, these residents understood that certain topographical features or weather conditions could increase the likelihood of slides. This combined knowledge contributed to the notion that some sites were safer than others. But the nature of avalanches meant that even "safe" places could fail to protect people. An avalanche at the thirteen-year-old Highland Mary Mine in Colorado, a location at which no slide had previously been recorded, led one local journalist to despair, "This goes to show that nowhere in the deep gulches of the San Juan can safety be relied upon. The fact that a snowslide has never been known to occur at a particular locality is no guarantee of safety whatever."[12] Over time this attitude would change somewhat, as mountain workers became more confident in their ability to predict slides.

Furthermore, mining corporations often turned a blind eye to their role in environmental degradation and increasing avalanche danger. As early as 1871, concern led one reporter to write, "One species of vandalism practised [sic] in that canyon [Little Cottonwood] deserves the most severe and speedy remedy; it is the destruction of timber of which there is not any surplus." He remarked that the "government ought to step in with its strong arm and save the timber to be used in developing the many mines in that district. If the present destructive policy is pursued, very soon the want of timber will be a serious question."[13] Beyond vanishing timber supplies, many observers avowed that the frequency of snowslides in the Little Cottonwood Canyon was directly connected to clear-cutting practices. An article published in 1885 in the *Deseret Evening News* critiqued the territory's abuse of its timber resources without thought for the future. The author suggested a system of replanting to replenish the supply, as well as to temper the climate, prevent erosion, and retain moisture. He went on to argue that Switzerland should serve as a role model; there, "the Government has very successfully experimented in forest growing as a means to reduce the fury and destructiveness of mountain torrents."[14] J. M. Goodwin, a writer for *Overland Monthly*, concurred that clear-cutting caused the horrible snowslides in both Little and Big Cottonwood Canyons. He wrote that thick forests once covered the mountainsides. Years of cutting timber to use in the mine tunnels had left the slopes denuded. He argued that this condition increased the size and frequency of snowslides. He estimated that at least 175 people had died in the canyon as a result of avalanches.[15] The connection was recognized in Colorado, too. Mountain resident James Hastings remarked that in the early 1870s, "In logging off the pine, sometimes the loggers were greedy and cut too close on the mountainside and then, when a Chinook blew for a day or two, the snow and more or less scenery, would come down on us."[16] He argued that if the loggers had left the timber alone, slide danger would have decreased.

In spite of the seemingly obvious connection between logging practices and avalanches, mine employers did little to change their methods. The financial risks that companies assumed when they invested in places such as Alta led them to put profit and output above worker safety both below and above ground, and better forestry techniques remained elusive. For example, a style of timbering to support the underground tunnels, invented by the superintendent of the Emma Mine at Alta, involved a complicated crosshatch system of reinforcement.[17] This infrastructure required an exceptional amount of timber, and woodcutters continued to strip bare the hillsides around Alta.[18]

As elsewhere in the Mountain West, in the San Juans and the Wasatch, the arrival of hard-rock mining altered work relationships for the many who became wage earners in the new corporate mines. Instead of bringing an abrupt end to independent mining, corporate mines employing dozens of workers and small claims run by two or three men often existed side by side.[19] Self-employed miners assumed the risks of inconsistent reward but had control over where they lived and when they worked. Those who worked for the mining companies hoped for a steadier income, although this was never assured, as companies routinely introduced pay cuts or reduced workers' hours when the price of silver dropped. At the same time, wageworkers increased their physical risks as they lost control over when and where they worked, and sometimes even where they lived, if they boarded in company housing.

The dangerous environment of the Mountain West complicated the relationship between risk and reward. The self-employed man could choose to stay away from his claim if he determined avalanche danger was too high after a storm, whereas the wageworker did not have that option. The independent prospector also could determine where to live, unlike company employees, who often lived in company bunkhouses and cabins. The Reverend James Joseph Gibbons wrote that although it should be "one of the first considerations of the miner to mark well the lay of the mountains, before he builds his cabin," the miner who lived in a company-built home lost this control.[20] The miner employed by a company therefore increased the physical risks he took in exchange for the hoped-for steady wage. These considerations contributed to ideas about acceptable risk, responsibility, and blame in Avalanche Country.

BUILDING COMMUNITY

In 1884, a Salt Lake City reporter for the *Deseret Evening News* tried to explain why men took work that risked their lives and limbs. The reason, he argued, had to do with people's pressing need for jobs. Where work existed, people followed, "impelled by choice or necessity, to perform it, let the risk attending its prosecution be ever so great." He hinted that industrial relations caused such need. Economic affairs meant "that many persons are compelled almost to enter the jaws of death to earn the means of a living."[21] But the preventative actions of Mountain West miners, such as forming unions and aid societies, suggested that they resisted seeing themselves as helpless victims at the mercy of their employers. Furthermore, the measures mountain workers took to reduce the risk of avalanches spoke to their perception that they had the power to wrest some control over their work and living spaces.

In the San Juans, miners organized in the early 1880s. Their unions represented the most important institutions that they built to bargain with their employers about unsatisfactory work conditions. Their understanding of fair wages was balanced against their perceptions of the risks they encountered, a connection recognized by Father Gibbons. He stressed, "That the miners are a class who are deserving of high wages is evident to any one who reflects upon the dangers and hardships to which they are subjected."[22] The San Juan miners modeled their union constitution and bylaws on those written by the Comstock miners in Nevada in the 1860s. Establishing a minimum wage became their primary goal, but they also concerned themselves with helping sick or injured miners and their families. Like other unions formed by industrial workers, the miners' unions provided help where the companies' minimal legal responsibilities ended.

The shift to industrial work in the Mountain West happened somewhat differently than in the established eastern towns, largely because of the boom–bust nature of mining towns and the transience of the residents who came and went based on employment opportunities. Transience meant unstable populations, but it also meant certain practices and knowledge about the region circulated rapidly. Unions, emigrant aid societies, family and friends in other towns, church services, and recreation all brought people together. As labor historian Elizabeth Jameson put it, "Mobility in hard-rock mining did not bring isolation and anomie so much as rapid diffusion of shared histories, values, and social institutions."[23] All miners faced the same dangers in the mines, and thus, "They based their cooperation in the understanding that everyone's safety was interdependent."[24] Because state laws privileged corporations' rights, miners relied on work practices to promote safety. Experienced miners passed their knowledge to new hires along with their belief in solidarity.[25]

Accommodation of environmental hazards became part of the workers' experience in the mountains, too. In Colorado, for example, corporate failure to protect miners was highlighted in a newspaper article published in 1887, which described the death of a silver miner in an avalanche at work. Another miner wrote a letter to the local paper about his friend's death. He implored that "no risks should be taken during or after a big storm," when the new snow increased the chances of a slide. Furthermore, he believed that "buildings should not be put up where there is the least danger of slides." The miner added, "We believe that the Colorado Legislature should pass a law making it a penal offense for mining superintendents who have buildings put up . . . where there is a possibility of a slide sweeping it away."[26] According to this miner, men could both predict and avoid avalanches, thereby preventing tragedies. It is important to note that this showed that over the course of the decade, residents' convictions about their ability to predict slides had increased. This editorial writer saw the law as an appropriate corrective to corporate negligence and an answer to the dangers imposed by avalanches.

The persistence of snow problems meant that nearly twenty years later, a 1906 editorial printed in the *Silverton Standard* called for a state law that would allow mining counties to hire an inspector whose job description included protecting people and property from avalanches. The paper, having consulted with "practical mining men," believed that the community supported such actions. Furthermore, the journalist decreed that the greater society, which already supported horticultural inspectors, cattle inspectors, and mine-safety inspectors, should also endorse legislation that protected lives and property from "the deadly avalanche." Even though no precedent for legislation that protected miners from natural disasters existed, such a pursuit would prove not only practical but necessary in the mountains. The editorial added, "Were a commission given plenary powers in the location of such plants both capital and lives would be guarded by the wisdom of experience instead of the immature judgment of tenderfoot M.E.'s [mining engineers] knowing and caring nothing about snow conditions."[27] A week later, a follow-up piece addressed the issue of natural disasters and insisted that, unlike tornadoes that "no human agency may tell when or where the funnel-shaped cloud may visit its wrath nor any human power avert it," men could guard against avalanche danger. The editorial concluded that a commission "would make mining safer and more profitable," equaling a win for both workers and companies.[28]

By the turn of the century, miners in California, like their counterparts in Colorado, held strong beliefs about what conditions caused slides. In Plumas, residents of the district's "deep canons or ravines" feared avalanches most of all. When they felt conditions looked especially dangerous, one contemporary source explained, they would put on their snowshoes and travel to "the nearest town or domicile there to wait until the snow had ceased falling and has settled so as not to be dangerous."[29] California miners' actions showed they possessed knowledge of slides that led them to identify conditions that were especially perilous and to move to safer locations to avoid danger. In the 1890s, disasters like a snowslide that covered part of Sierra City and "buried a number of its inhabitants" served as a reminder that even the precautions they took would not always protect them, a reality that kept communities vigilant and highly conscious of the risks they took daily in the winter.[30]

Rather than perceiving risk as an individual responsibility, most miners viewed safety as a communal obligation. Disaster response in Alta and the San Juans demonstrates how this sense of solidarity permeated beyond the workplace and how coping with avalanches became a way of life in Little Cottonwood Canyon and other sections of the Mountain West.[31] Slides often rushed uneventfully down the mountainsides, but even these harmless slides were reminders of the ones that hit boarding houses, other residences, and entire sections of town.[32] Rescue efforts during catastrophic avalanches often reached Herculean proportions. For example, in Little Cottonwood Canyon in 1872, after a slide engulfed a party of sleighs, including teamsters and passengers, two hundred men arrived at the scene to dig for survivors.[33]

Although in the case of such disasters today, we would call out search-and-rescue helicopters and avalanche dogs, community-based rescues became the primary response in the nineteenth century, in part because no formal emergency networks existed. Events of the winters of 1883 to 1884 and 1884 to 1885 in Alta highlight how residents dealt with catastrophes. The season of 1883 to 1884 began usually enough, with snow shutting down railroad service on December 11 for the winter.[34] Charles Penrose, editor of the *Deseret Evening News*, mused hopefully that traditional signs, such as thin husks on the annual corn crop and gentle southeasterly winds, pointed toward a temperate winter season.[35] The months passed without major tragedy in the Little Cottonwood Canyon. Then, on March 4, a blizzard that lasted for three days began.[36] Reports of snowslides in nearby Laketown and Park City came in the news.[37]

On Monday, March 10, word reached Salt Lake City that a horrendous avalanche had killed twelve people at the Emma Mine near Alta on Friday night. The slide, nearly half a mile wide, had buried the blacksmith's shop at the mouth of the mine. The group buried had gathered there in preparation to enter the tunnel, where they intended to spend the night in the only place they perceived as safe from slides. A group of four, also headed for the safety of the mine, barely escaped death because the sole female member of the party had asked them to stop and rest. While the party paused, the avalanche passed inches away and obliterated the trail ahead of them.

Rescuers immediately began to hunt for the victims. After they found most of the bodies, a group of twenty-two men made the arduous journey to Salt Lake City to request help in removing the dead for burial in the city. Because of the extreme conditions, it took them three hours just to go the first four miles down the canyon.[38]

Although many mountain towns did not have a city nearby from which to seek help, Alta's inhabitants turned to Salt Lake City residents when slides overwhelmed their ability to address the destruction. At a meeting on March 11, citizens of Salt Lake City gathered at the federal courthouse to collect funds and sign up volunteers to help remove the bodies from Alta.[39] A special train carried the recovery crew within eight miles of Alta, at which point it was forced to stop because of heavy snow. The men then broke a trail up to the mine to retrieve the dead. When they arrived they discovered the town covered with snow up to the rooftops. Avalanches had choked the many gulches and ravines that cut down through the canyon's walls. Volunteers tied the eleven recovered bodies to sleds and pulled them down to the train. The train took the corpses back to Salt Lake City for an inquest and burial arrangements. The final victim, Willard Stevenson, remained lost under the snow.[40]

The next winter, avalanches again upset the order of life in Alta, but with more permanent results. On Friday night, February 13, 1885, a wall of snow inundated the town and its citizens. In Salt Lake City, the news caused "the greatest fever of excitement it has experienced in years." Readers took in the news of the worst snowslide ever to strike the mountain town.[41] The slide, almost a mile long, came in the middle of the night, so the totality of the disaster remained obscured until daylight revealed the utter devastation.[42] Only seven buildings escaped destruction, and at the Emma Mine the avalanche crushed the tramway, railroad office, ore house, and other structures. As news filtered down from the canyon, Utah governor Eli Murray chaired a meeting that aimed to organize fifty or sixty men to go help the people of Alta. Plenty came forward. Another committee organized to raise funds for the victims and for burials.[43]

Thirteen people died in the slide, and many more were injured.[44] This slide forced residents to reassess their choices for disaster response. Terrified that another slide might strike, forty-one of Alta's residents did not wait for the rescue party from Salt Lake City and began the trek down the canyon to safety. They brought with them twelve dead and two injured strapped on sleds. About halfway down the canyon they ran into the rescue party. With the rescuers' help they continued the evacuation and took a special train from Wasatch into Salt Lake City. A second group of rescuers reached Alta several days later and assisted those left in Alta who wanted to leave. Of the 150 men, women, and children living in or near Alta at the time of the slide, only 12 chose to stay.[45]

The decision by Congress to demonetize silver in 1873, making gold the only metal to back U.S. dollars, did not immediately slow production in Alta. But as the mines began to play out and the price of silver fell through the 1880s, so, too, did Alta's population. Some residents chose to rebuild, but Alta never regained its vitality after the avalanche of 1885. Many chose to live there in the summer only, and the Emma Mine shut down during the snowy months. Only a few remained to mine silver into the twentieth century.

Other examples of community response to disaster come from Colorado. Independent miners and those who worked for companies had a sense of kinship that compelled them to undertake dangerous search-and-rescue operations there, too.[46] In the winter of 1890 to 1891, a writer for the *Silverton Standard* declared, "The snow slides have been simply fearful, nothing of the kind has been seen for the last 12 years. The oldest timer in this district never saw anything of the kind."[47] The temperatures dropped so low that some miners found their "great powder" (i.e., dynamite) too cold to ignite.[48] Billy Maher, a so-called oldtimer who practiced tricks such as sleeping with his breakfast potatoes to keep them from freezing, also had a habit of thawing out his great powder by the cabin's fire on frigid mornings. On February 25, he let the powder get too hot and it blew up in his face. His partner, a recent Italian immigrant, went for help. New to skiing, Maher's partner fell down every time he tried to use his skis. He finally stuck his hands in the toe straps, knelt on the boards, and crawled toward the Terrible Mine for help. It took him seven and a half hours to reach his destination, which was only a mile away.

Four men, more experienced on their skis, went to the cabin and retrieved Billy. On their way back to the Terrible a huge storm blew up and the men heard the horrible roar of a snowslide to their right. Scared and exhausted, they finally made it back to the Terrible. They expected to find four men from the Virginius Mine waiting there to carry out the second leg of the rescue mission to the hospital in Ouray, but the relief party never came. The four tired men from the Terrible carried their burden all the way to town.

The next day the rescue party returned up the mountain and chastised the men from the Virginius for not sending help. The accused protested, arguing that they had sent several men. It was at that point that "they all instinctively turned and looked down the mountain side. There they beheld the track of an awful snowslide and they knew the fate of the miners."[49] Maher died a few days later in the hospital. Almost everyone from the town turned out to pay respects. The funeral offered another avenue for individuals to support one another and praise the rescuers, reinforcing the actions of those who responded to winter disasters. When mourners came together, they built community around the sorrow and hardships they shared.

Miners risked their lives for each other, and group responsibility outweighed personal culpability. Even though the "Italian" could see that his partner would likely die, he made every effort to go for help. Rather than blaming Maher for his carelessness, the other miners-men who did not even work with him-came to his aid. The miners at both the Terrible and Virginius agreed to help, knowing full well the risks that winter travel entailed. Maher obviously put himself in danger with his activities, yet his neighbors went unhesitatingly to his assistance. The men's critical attitude toward the miners from the Virginius, before understanding what had happened to the rescue party, spoke to the participation expected of all when others needed help. They assigned blame to the men they believed acted inappropriately, not to Maher, who was only participating in a common practice of warming explosives by his fire when the accident happened.

In another case, in 1902, a massive snowslide obliterated the Liberty Bell

Mine above Telluride, Colorado, demolishing many buildings and burying two engineers. A rescue party of miners was in the process of digging out the men "when another avalanche descended, burying nearly twenty of the rescuers." By the end of the day "no less than six masses of snow came down . . . and the bodies of the victims were not recovered until several months afterward. . . . In all twenty-three men were killed at this place by slides that day."[50] Even after some died digging out the victims, rescuers did not stop looking for the buried, who by all odds were already dead.[51]

Across the Rockies in the 1880s and 1890s, men risked their lives to dig out slide victims, and the rescue missions that helped Maher and avalanche victims characterized community actions after slides struck. The Homestake Mine near Leadville, Colorado, was the site of two such efforts. In 1881, concern over a miner who had not picked up his mail in several weeks sent fifty men from Leadville to Homestake on skis; the mail was so important that if someone did not pick it up others assumed something was wrong. Their assumption proved correct when they found four men dead in a cabin, asphyxiated by an avalanche. Four years later, in 1885, Homestake miners' failure to collect their mail again incited worry. Two men who went to investigate found all three buildings at the camp obliterated by a slide. This time about one hundred volunteers converged to look for survivors and bodies. The rescuers found ten dead. They took the bodies to Leadville, where community members donated money for their funerals and burials. The community contributed leftover funds to the families of the victims, again speaking to the shared sense of community responsibility when disaster struck.[52]

BEYOND CATASTROPHE

Shared experiences in the Mountain West included more than just dealing with tragedy. Intra- and intercommunity social events also brought miners together and created bonds. Well known are the saloons, brothels, and gambling halls that miners visited in their free time, but they participated in other recreational activities, too. When not at work, for example, miners across the Mountain West participated in games of chance and would bet on practically anything, a habit that led historian Gunther Peck, in his study of Virginia City, Nevada, to argue that "prize fights and gambling contests . . . formed important elements of an alternative working-class culture . . . that venerated chance and limited economic gains, rather than rational capital accumulation. Risks were shared rather than calculated in these spontaneous contests, as were their consequences."[53] Ski races offered a similar venue for risk takers to bet against one another while at the same time exhibiting one of the most important survival skills in their communities. The snow, which sometimes brought death, also created a playground. Ski races and ski clubs became the focus of many workers' time off during the winter months.

Ski races, which involved prize money and betting opportunities, began in California, and became popular in other mountain places as well. While miners learned to ski to travel, the adoption of this activity for leisure time brought excitement and gave miners a reason to gather together as well as display an essential skill. Those who became experts had the opportunity to show off to their fellow miners at ski meets around their districts. In 1870, "Snowshoe" Thompson wowed hundreds of spectators when he appeared at the top of a hill and gave "one of his wild High-Sierra Whoops." He seemed to fly down the mountain on his skis, shaming the other participants who watched him in awe.[54] According to a piece that appeared in *California Illustrated Magazine* in 1894, the miners who lived near Plumas in the Sierras "live together like members of a large family, thus enjoying the association and counsel of one another," gathering at one another's houses in the long evenings to play music and games.[55] But their favorite pastime in the winter was ski racing. Each town had its own club and would gather contributions to pay to the snowshoer who made it fastest down a designated route. A notice would go out, and "great is the excitement when there appears upon the bulletin board at the post office the notice announcing the event."[56] By this time various concoctions–referred to as dope–spread on the bottoms of skis to increase speed and keep the snow from sticking had become common. One notice began, "Dope is King! Dope is King!" It then listed the place, times, and purse for each of the races.[57] All those talented on their skis would practice until the big day, when each club would choose its best skiers to compete.

Similarly, "in December of 1880, three Norwegian miners working near Silverton, Colorado, challenged anyone in the United States to a race."[58] A few years later, the people of Crested Butte sponsored a ski race. Racers formed a club "for the object of encouraging snow-shoeing and all other winter sports."[59] The competition began on February 22, 1886, and first prize was $37—roughly $900 in today's dollars. Racers came from up to twenty miles away and vied for the fastest time down the mountainside.[60]

Gunnison held a race on March 5, drawing between twenty-five and thirty participants from White Pine, Pitkin, Crested Butte, Gothic, Schofield, and Crystal City. Schools closed for the event, and the Rio Grande Railroad "ran a special train up the course for the benefit of the spectators."[61] The ski races in Crested Butte and Gunnison proved so popular that towns such as Irwin, Gothic, and Schofield held races that same winter. The average race had twenty participants. The success of the races spurred plans for the following year, including a "two or three days carnival . . . and races of various kinds."[62]

Other towns across the Mountain West held ski races or formed social clubs around skiing, and communities bragged about the skills of their local skiers. In 1874, Altaites claimed their "snow-shoe experts . . . we feel proud to state" were as skilled as "can be found anywhere in the Territory. We have two or three among our snow-shoeists who are open for a challenge for any amount; and we have no hesitation in saying that if accepted Alta will win the 'laurels.' "[63] The Alta snowshoe club had a chance to prove its claims when it held a race a week later.[64] The few women in Alta also participated in this "main amusement of the Altaites" and could be seen about town "enjoying the exhilarating exercise."[65] Ouray's Mount Sneffles Snowshoe Club posed for photographs in 1887, as did the Lady Skiers of Breckenridge in 1889. In 1913, Steamboat Springs held its first winter carnival and celebrated activities such as ski racing and shooting from skis. The mostly local participants and observers came together to break the monotony of the winter and engage in friendly competition.[66]

The thrilling races often ended in injury-causing crashes, but they did not entail the deadly risks mountain residents confronted regularly. Furthermore, although not explicitly stated, the honing of skills in play that mimicked skills required in life prepared mountain residents for the challenges they faced as they went about their work. Even so, the incorporation of skiing into leisure time activities showed how completely environmental realities had permeated life in the mountains.

By 1902, most miners had become enmeshed in an industrial work culture that valued solidarity and mutualism. The process of moving to the mountains, learning to live and work there, and the building of communities led mountain people to formulate relationships with their environment that moved beyond dualistic notions like man versus nature or emerging bourgeois ideas about the sublimity of nature. Instead, mountain people began to develop communities built on trans-local exchanges of knowledge that infused their work, home, and leisure time. In doing so they also built expectations about personal and group responsibility in terms of disaster.

As newcomers, mountain miners, mailmen, preachers, and residents survived, coped, and responded to environmental conditions and disasters, they demonstrated how the mountain environment influenced individual and group actions. The mountain environment did not necessarily elicit unprecedented responses from European Americans; still, the difficult environment both intensified and promulgated actions not regularly required back home.[67] Vitally, the arrival of corporate mining and the settling of communities made knowledge of environmental hazards a critical component of life in the Mountain West. Like the trappers before them, mountain people in the second half of the nineteenth century adapted and updated methods of dealing with winter problems. Over time, with the introduction of industrial work, ways of knowing nature grew increasingly complex as mountain people found themselves losing control over when they worked and where they lived. The industrial process did not end winter problems—instead it magnified them—and dealing with a dangerous environment became an entrenched part of the work customs of trainmen who worked on the mountain lines, too.

Figure 1. Miner traveling on skis to the goldfields in La Porte, Plumas County, California, 1860s. His skis, pole, and pack are typical gear for a mountain miner. Courtesy of University of Utah digital archives

Figure 2. In 1886, men (some wearing sunglasses) posed with the bodies of miners either recovered from a snowslide or killed when the roof of their cabin collapsed because of heavy snow accumulation at the Homestake Mine near Leadville, Colorado. Courtesy of Denver Public Library digital collections; X-60005 (DPL)

Figure 3. The mining town of Silver Plume, Colorado, is situated below
tree line at about 9,000 feet; but there are not many trees left standing in
this image, taken around 1890. Mountain residents generally agreed that
deforestation led to increased danger from snowslides. Courtesy of Denver
Public Library digital collections; H-370 (DPL)

Figure 4. July 1888: A mule train carrying mail pauses before passing through a tunnel cut through a slide on the toll road from Ouray to Silverton, Colorado.

Figure 5. Drawing of riding the rails through Little Cottonwood Canyon, Utah, 1880s–1890s. Courtesy of University of Utah digital archives

Figure 6. Taken on July 3, 1885, this photograph of Alta, Utah, shows men
in front of structures destroyed by an avalanche, with deforested Rustler
Mountain in the background. Courtesy of University of Utah digital archives

Figure 7. Aerial tramway buckets, like this one in San Juan County, Colorado, 1880s–1910, delivered supplies to mines on steep slopes and carried ore down the mountain in places where it was impractical to build roads. Courtesy of Denver Public Library digital collections; X-60701 (DPL)

Figure 9 *(above)*. The Liberty Bell Mine sat west of Telluride, Colorado, in the San Juan Range. This picture (circa 1890) shows the shaft house, aerial tramway, and boardinghouse. Stumps are all that remain of the trees that once protected the boardinghouse from slides. Courtesy of Denver Public Library digital collections; X-62359 (DPL)

Figure 8 *(opposite)*. Men sometimes used the aerial tramway buckets for transportation to and from the mines, as seen here in San Juan County, Colorado, in the early twentieth century. Note the reinforced tram tower and the steep mountains in the background: both hint at the likelihood of snowslides in the winter months. Courtesy of Denver Public Library digital collections; X-62249 (DPL)

Figure 10. This early twentieth-century image captures a Denver and Rio Grande railway locomotive making its way through a deep snow cut somewhere in San Juan County, Colorado. Courtesy of Denver Public Library digital collections; GB-8148 (DPL)

Figure 11. Man stands atop the "Saguache Slide" near Silverton, Colorado.
Courtesy of Denver Public Library digital collections; Z-5469 (DPL)

Figure 12. This snowshed was built just west of Alpine Tunnel on the Denver, South Park, and Pacific's route through the mountains of central Colorado. Logs were propped against the outside of the snowshed to reinforce the structure against repeated avalanches. Courtesy of Denver Public Library digital collections; C-163 (DPL)

Figure 13. Crushed building, possibly the section house run by Marcella
Doyle, who lost six of eight children in a slide at Woodstock, Colorado, in
1884. Courtesy of Denver Public Library digital collections; Z-2768 (DPL)

Figure 14. Shovelers, many of them volunteers, dug out the bodies at the site of the 1910 slide at Rogers Pass that killed fifty-eight railway workers east of Revelstoke, British Columbia. Courtesy of Revelstoke Railway Museum; no call number (RRM)

Figure 15. Shovelers and rotary plow work to clear the slide at the site of the 1910 Rogers Pass slide. Courtesy of Revelstoke Railway Museum; no call number (RRM)

Figure 16. The Bailets Hotel in Wellington, Washington, 1910. Note the deep snow surrounding the hotel and the charred stumps and trees behind it—conditions that increased slide danger significantly. Courtesy of University of Washington archives; CUR 724 (U of W)

Figure 17. In this case a snowshed near Wellington, Washington, withstood a 1910 avalanche, but the end was blocked by snow and debris. Courtesy of University of Washington archives; CUR 735 (U of W)

Figure 18. Men struggle to remove bodies tangled in snow, trees, and twisted metal in the aftermath of the powerful slide that struck two trains at Wellington, Washington, in 1910. Courtesy of University of Washington archives; CUR 719 (U of W)

Figure 19. This Great Northern rotary snowplow was no match for the slide that knocked it off the tracks at Wellington, Washington, in 1910. Courtesy of University of Washington archives; CUR 717 (U of W)

Figure 20. An avalanche killed nearly seventy people, including workers
building an aerial tramway, at Chilkoot Pass, Alaska Territory, on April 3,
1898; the massive slide covered the valley floor.

RAILWAY WORKERS AND MOUNTAIN TOWNS: 1870-1910

So sudden was the disaster that the men had no time to make for safety, and died an awful death, being crushed by the mass of ice that thundered down upon them.

—*Revelstoke Mail-Herald*, March 5, 1910

We would consider a place safe where in our history there hadn't a slide come theretofore.

—W. R. Smith, 1910

I N 1898, MERRIDAN HOWARD WROTE IN *PEARSON'S MAGAZINE* about the heroic efforts made by the Mountain West's railway workers to keep the tracks clear, in even the worst winter storms:

It is truly, a royal foe . . . that the railroad men have to encounter in the mountains. . . . There are in America thousands of men whose sole employment during the snow months is to wage war on this colossal antagonist. It is exciting work, a life that involves the most stupendous hardships and unceasing risk.[1]

Winter work on the rails, in Howard's opinion, was not just a job; it was a war against a daunting enemy undertaken by American men willing to put their lives on the line. By comparing railroad work to the battlefield, Howard conjured up striking images for readers, tying the themes of man versus nature with images of righteous battle and American might.

In another, more florid example of stories that pitted man against nature, the popular publication *Munsey's Magazine* printed a piece that described railway workers as near godlike. The article described the winter of 1898 to 1899, which tested railway workers in Colorado's High Country as never before. Heavy snows shut down the railroads in late winter, cutting mountain residents off from critical supplies. Writer Francis Lynde reported that "the situation in the mountain towns along the lines soon became alarming." The three main railroad companies based in Denver joined together and hired men armed with shovels and ice picks to "break trail" so that the rotary plow, "the warship of the snow seas," could come through.[2] Even worse than working through the snow and ice, frequent avalanches left the men on the lines without supplies. Eventually the rails were clear enough of debris that the rotary plows could get through and bring food to the hungry mountain communities. Although Lynde proclaimed that the marvelous technology of the rotary plow certainly deserved credit, he wrote that the men who persevered under harsh conditions should be praised above all:

> From the nearer Rockies to the farther Sierras the winter night's tale of the railway is an epic of heroism; and when its Homer shall arise to write it we shall have a nobler Iliad than that which sings the war of the Greeks and Trojans. For the heroes of old fought with flesh and blood, and to slay their fellow creatures; but these men of the mountains battle with grim winter in its fiercest moods, with pitiless storms and perils uncharted, and this not to slay, but to stay alive.[3]

Even as plows were developed through the years that were better equipped to handle the extreme amount of snow, Lynde proclaimed that men's muscles and spirits remained an important tool in battling the elements. As Howard had similarly written, Lynde touched on popular themes that defined manhood in terms of physical action and bravery. Particularly embedded in American thought at the time was a belief that the frontier lifestyle had inculcated in its populace desirable characteristics such as independence, superior physical strength, and integrity. People in urban areas seemed in serious danger of losing these important American attributes, according to the prevailing view, and many "had begun to fear that mechanization was unnerving even the most affluent Americans."[4] As a consequence, tales of hearty westerners reassured urban dwellers that technology did not have to undermine masculine traits, that examples of heroism based on physical bravery still existed, and that American men of strength and fortitude still shaped the nation.

But how closely did these stories match the actions of the real-life men who worked the mountain lines? Cutting through the flowery rhetoric and reconstructing the experiences of the railway workers reveals a world of heroes for certain; it also shows that skilled workers' knowledge of their surroundings had developed over time. Like the trappers, explorers, emigrants, and miners before them, mountain railway workers contended with an environment that brought severe challenges. Work and environment became intertwined in Avalanche Country as mountain railway workers exchanged and built knowledge that affected their work customs, gained experience that colored their perceptions of risk, and survived disasters that influenced how they understood responsibility after a tragedy occurred.

SNOW PROBLEMS ON THE LINES

Building, repairing and keeping rail lines open in winter proved a challenge across the Mountain West. In 1866, a Chinese laborer working on the transcontinental railroad in the Sierras commented: " 'The snow slides carried away our camps and we lost a good many men in those slides. Many of them we did not find until the next season when the snow melted.' "[5] The number of Chinese workers killed by slides remains elusive, but the interference in the building and maintenance of tracks in all the major ranges because of snow is well documented. Alta, Utah, is an example of the kind of winter climate workers had to face: It was not unusual to see the weather in the canyon change rapidly, going from bright sunshine to intense storms that dropped several feet of snow at a time within a matter of hours.[6] Common throughout the region were storms like one described in 1874: "On Thursday we were favored with one of those favorite snow storms which continued for two days, and caused our roads to be blocked up for the time being."[7] These conditions first held up construction, and later they would often halt the flow of goods and people through the mountains.

Although engineers made every effort to plan routes that avoided the worst avalanche paths, they could not always predict the safest routes or avoid all the danger zones. When the Denver and Rio Grande Railway built its Telluride route, it avoided a known slide path. But much to the company's surprise, a slide traveled along a new pathway and swept twenty-five loaded freight cars into a canyon soon after the line opened.[8] Railroad engineers had chosen the rail route based on their knowledge that slides often traveled the same paths winter after winter, but they could not prepare for erratic slab avalanches that were less predictable than the loose snowslides that came down gullies or the cornice-fall avalanches that fell from windswept ridges. Similarly, when the Denver, South Park, and Pacific (DSP&P) Railway Company began extending a narrow-gauge line to Gunnison, Colorado, early in 1880, the steep mountainsides and slides gave them more problems than they had anticipated. The rugged terrain necessitated the construction of Alpine Tunnel, a huge and expensive project that held up the completion of the line until September 1882.

Railroads built snowsheds to protect the tracks, a method of defense invented by engineers working for the Central Pacific Railroad in response to frequent avalanches that held up trains in the Sierras.[9] Snowsheds, usually built of wood, covered sections of track that experienced slides regularly.[10] These sheds were built so that the slide, in theory, would flow over the roof, protecting the line from blockage or at least leaving an opening through the slide for trains to pass through. But even with tunnels and snowsheds, avalanches and heavy snows shut down lines repeatedly.[11] The snow could be so deep that one man traveling on foot (or possibly skis) from the Elk Mountain district to Gunnison in the winter of 1883 to 1884 used the tops of telegraph poles to guide his progress. When he got tired he sat on the cross-arms to rest.[12]

Similar issues arose in Canada when building the transcontinental railroad. James Ross, the engineer in charge of building the Canadian Pacific Railway (CPR) through the Rocky and Selkirk Mountains, wrote to headquarters in 1883: "I find the snow-slides on the Selkirks much more serious than I anticipated." Underfinancing slowed the project, and the workers had not seen a paycheck in a while, a situation that led to a disgruntled workforce prone to drinking on the job. But more than inebriation, the fear of frequent slides made the men hard to control. Ross wrote: "The great trouble we are labouring under at present is that the men are frightened. Seven have already been buried."[13] He requested that management immediately send an engineer who had more experience with snowslides to assist at the treacherous Rogers Pass section of the CPR's Mountain Division. By 1884, workers, mostly Chinese men brought from California and China, finished the final portion of the line through Rogers Pass.[14] In 1885, the last spike was pounded in Craigellachie, about thirty miles west of Revelstoke. In the next few years the persistent threat of avalanches led the CPR to build 31 snowsheds, a total of 4 miles in length, through the pass.[15]

Rail lines developed other structural methods to protect the tracks and trains. They erected timber "glances," or snow fences, upslope from the tracks that deflected avalanches by shunting the flow of snow away from the rail line.[16] In British Columbia, the CPR built separate summer and winter tracks, the summer track left open to the elements and the winter track covered with a snowshed.[17] These constructions could arguably save companies money in the long run by cutting back on the number of shovelers hired and the cost of repairing damage caused to snowplows over the course of the winter clearing snow off the tracks.[18]

These kinds of snow problems affected rail lines in Washington's Cascade Range, too. The Northern Pacific (NP) struggled first to build its line through these mountains. In 1872, NP engineers cautioned that terrible slides assaulted the passes and that conditions would require at least twenty-five to thirty miles of snowsheds along any route.[19] Financial difficulties and indecision about the best route meant that the NP did not complete its line through the Cascades until 1887. Undeterred by his competitor's problems, Great Northern (GN) president James J. Hill remained convinced that extending his line through the Cascades would increase the company's profits. As early as 1887, Major Albert Bowman Rogers, who had chosen the route for the CPR through the Selkirk Mountains in 1881 to 1882, warned Hill that slides in the Cascades presented an even more serious problem than they had in Canada. Even so, Hill hired John F. Stevens, who surveyed a route over what became known as Stevens Pass. Workers completed the GN to the Pacific Ocean in 1893, but continued improving the line. In 1897, construction began on Cascade Tunnel so that trains could go under rather than through a severe avalanche zone.[20] But even after the tunnel was completed, trains passing through the tunnel continued to face peril as snowslides regularly blocked either end of the passageway. Avalanches also became worse after fires destroyed stands of timber that had previously offered some protection to the line, and in the winter of 1897 to 1898, up to twenty feet of snow fell, requiring the GN to hire at least 1,500 shovelers to dig out the rails.

Railroads also developed equipment to deal with snow. Trains attached a plow called "a 'gouger'; a strongly built box car with a huge flat scraper at the prow set low to run under the snow like a great wedge, with hinged wings at the sides to widen the breach when it was once fairly opened."[21] A typical "snow outfit" for a train consisted of a snow train (six engines), the front engine equipped with the snowplow. Hooked to the back were two cabooses, or "good vans," carrying fifty men, armed with picks and shovels, whose job was to dig out particularly troublesome blockades or the plow when it got mired in snow.[22] When snow blocked the rails, a string of locomotives would back up; then "the engineer of the leading engine would whistle 'off brakes,' and the mass of iron and steel would hurl itself into the obstruction with all the momentum that could be developed in the mile start."[23] Not surprisingly, accidents occurred regularly while snowbucking—the name used to describe their plowing technique. Drifts of snow might appear soft but often hid solid blocks of ice. When the snowplow at the front of the train hit the ice while going full steam, it had the potential to ruin the engine and crush the workers on board.[24] For example, in 1876, near Truckee, California, eight attached engines "dashed into a slide pack . . . smashing the plow, disabling every one of the engines, and killing or maiming more than half of the crews."[25] Accidents like these kept men alert to the added risks of winter work.

Over time, the railroads improved their methods of snow removal. The rotary plow, another North American invention, reduced the number of calamities by churning through the snow rather than slamming into the drifts.[26] The rotary plow, "an immense auger which is revolved at a high speed by a steam engine within the car," had a blower chamber with a spout that shot the snow out to the sides of the track.[27] The rotary allowed men to clear the track more efficiently and with greater safety than the gouger had. Even so, slides often left behind densely packed masses of snow, ice, rocks, branches, and other debris. The rotary could not always handle the mess, and rail companies still needed to hire shovelers to dig slides out by hand. Unskilled laborers, many recent immigrants from Europe and Asia, usually filled these seasonal jobs.

Overall, although the railway companies constructed defenses to protect their lines and ensure that the trains ran year-round, the methods were imperfect. The railway workers bore the brunt of the risk, and the career railway men who devoted their work lives to jobs on the Mountain Divisions—the sections of rail that crisscrossed the Rockies, Sierras, and Cascades—became experts at reading the terrain and predicting snowslides. For them, the constant exposure to danger would influence the development of their workplace practices and blur the line between workplace hazards and outdoor spaces.

The presence of the railroad did not end mountain residents' problems during the winter; in fact, it was quite the opposite. Industries' desire to access the mining towns of the Mountain West, the need for reliable transcontinental routes, and technological advancements that made rail travel possible in extreme terrain, brought more people into and through the region. This included the industrial workforce needed to operate the trains and maintain the tracks. As a result, the populations of mountain towns grew with the arrival of the rail lines. In Canada, the transcontinental line contributed to the growth of British Columbia, where the population roughly doubled every ten years after the completion of the line in 1885, until 1910.[28] More people in the mountains, however, meant more people in harm's way. For them "the snow was a foe."[29] One engineer recalled that his time in the western mountains "was one to make a railway man long for the 'soft snaps' [versus a cold snap, one supposes] of New England." As the Reverend Joseph James Gibbons in Colorado put it, "The farmer watches the winter's storm with joy, while the miner," or railroad worker, "fearing the snowslide and the precipice, dreads its approach."[30] Winter marked the onset of a perilous season fraught with storms, snow, and avalanches.

Technology did not necessarily improve safety for those working for the railroads and other industrial jobs. Historians have estimated that "by the last quarter of the nineteenth century, the number of industrial accidents had grown enormously. After 1900, it is estimated that industrial accidents caused 35,000 deaths and 2,000,000 injuries every year in the United States."[31] Invariably the companies attributed the deaths to "acts of God" or the workers' "carelessness."[32] The railroads' refusal to take responsibility for worker safety included both industrial accidents and injuries attributed to natural disasters. At a time when companies had little legal responsibility for worker safety, trainmen relied on their skill and good work practices to protect themselves. Although it might seem counterintuitive, skilled railway workers sometimes objected to safety improvements because they worried such protections would devalue their skills and leave them replaceable. For example, couplers—individuals who added and disconnected railcars—had a high rate of injury and death from being crushed between cars, yet they did not endorse automatic couplers because the new mechanisms would undermine their expertise. Any value a railway worker lost because a machine or unskilled worker could do the job just as well undercut his union's ability to petition for higher pay, shorter hours, or medical care.[33] Many skilled trainmen preferred to rely on the work practices and safety measures they had developed over time, some especially singular to Avalanche Country, rather than relinquish control over their workplace.

Mountain railroad towns had a stability not found in the boom-and-bust mining towns, because of the steady demand for skilled workers and the regular schedules of the trains. Career railway men contributed to building these communities, raised their families there, and simultaneously developed strategies to cope with the risks they faced at their jobs, including a list of conditions that led to slides. The stability of the community meant that their understanding of slides became firmly entrenched and experienced workers used their knowledge to enforce work practices that impelled men to work under the worst conditions, developed an identity that was connected to the pride they took in their risky jobs, and faithfully believed in their methods of predicting avalanches. Their encounters with slides and one another reinforced the bonds they built and their knowledge of their environment, and the longer they worked for the railroads, the more committed they became to workplace practices that reduced risk as they worked with tons of metal and scalding steam in the midst of ferocious storms and slides.

REVELSTOKE, BRITISH COLUMBIA

Revelstoke, British Columbia, resembled other towns that grew out of the need to establish points along the lines where repairs and engine and crew changes were made. Railroad workers held a significant place in the economic and social structure in towns that existed mainly because of their strategic use to the railway, and by the late nineteenth century the residents of Revelstoke were familiar with the danger of slides.[34]

Revelstoke, situated in the Selkirk Mountains where the rail line crosses the Columbia River, was at one time home to many railway workers. Rogers Pass, approximately 40 miles east and nearly 3,000 feet higher than the town, became known as one of the most treacherous sections of rail along the transcontinental route. Runaway trains on steep sections, mudslides, avalanches, and up to thirty feet of snow a year made service in the region unreliable.[35] The Rogers Pass station and repair shops sat three miles east of the summit. By 1898, the station had earned such a bad reputation, due to its location at the bottom of a known avalanche chute, that most of the workers and operations there relocated to Revelstoke. By 1899, only a few railroad employees, including railroad agent/operator William Cator, his wife, and children Charlie and Ethel, lived permanently on the pass in the station that served as living space, boarding house, and center of operations. Shovel gangs also stayed on the pass as needed.[36]

On February 1, 1899, a terrible avalanche struck the station and roundhouse on the pass.[37] The slide destroyed buildings, and it took the lives of six people. Searchers found Cator and his family encased in snow and ice—his wife arrested in the act of baking (some accounts said a pie, others a cake). They uncovered the other victims halted in action by the wall of snow. Only local waitress Annie Berger and a man, Frank Vogel, who hid under the table when he heard the roar of the descending slide, survived. While the slide had come down a known route, it hit with unusual speed and force, and most in its path never had a chance of escape.[38] People in Revelstoke knew well the dangerous winter conditions that afflicted the CPR section of track in the Mountain Division; still, the loss of life shocked many. Others in the community, however, avowed that the dangers of that location were well known, as evidenced by the fact that the CPR had moved its major operations into town.[39] Some marveled that the death toll had not been worse: In a stroke of luck, engine trouble had delayed the train carrying CPR General Superintendent Richard Marpole and Superintendent Edward Duchesnay below the pass, and the shovel gangs had gone that night to dig out a slide at the Number Nineteen snowshed and had thereby escaped death from the icy mass.[40]

Regional papers commented on the deadly slides and celebrated the sacrifices made by those who served the national project of keeping a transcontinental route open year-round. The *Kootenay Mail*, a Revelstoke paper, discussed how railroad employees well knew that Rogers Pass experienced frequent snowslides, yet still they fulfilled their "duties" so that "East may meet West."[41] The presence of slides might "unnerve them for a little," but the railmen's jobs demanded they go to work, no matter the danger.[42] The paper also praised the acts of Marpole and Duchesnay, declaring that this most disastrous event on the CPR line had not unsettled the men: "Nothing that man could do was left undone by the company's staff . . . to mitigate its horror."[43] Describing the "western railroader—from superintendent to section hand"—as heroic and selfless, the paper suggested that railroaders, in their fight against the snow, answered a higher calling than the average man.

One could choose to look at these comments cynically as a disconnection between the boosterism of a local newspaper and the reality of the dangerous work the men did, but the newspaper coverage has more to tell. In journalistic and fictional accounts of westward expansion, the themes of manliness and duty were referenced frequently. Yet this characterization at times also reflected how experienced railroad workers understood their jobs.[44] Railway men in Revelstoke took great satisfaction in having special skills that countered job-related hazards, and like their brothers in the United States they had diligently fought for union recognition, shorter hours, and higher pay in acknowledgment of their expertise.[45] In the wake of the slide, the CPR admitted that establishing operations on the pass had been a bad decision and moved the station to a location where slides fell less frequently. They also built more snowsheds and moved the track into the middle of the canyon, away from the steep walls of the pass.[46] The 1899 slide reminded residents of the dangers of Rogers Pass, yet work went on as usual, a clue to how the men assessed risk. As later events revealed, railroad workers used their sense of duty and obligation and their knowledge of the environment to help explain why they worked under such hazardous conditions and to justify why they returned to their jobs after tragedy occurred.

WINTER OF 1910

By 1910, Revelstoke held an important place among the towns that dotted the CPR's Mountain Division rails. Citizens looked forward to the prosperous years ahead based on their prominent place on the transcontinental route. At least one resident even believed that Revelstoke was the most suitable location for a future provincial university, because "the proximity of large mountain streams assures abundant supply of the purest water."[47] Even more important, "From no other city of the province can there be seen such a magnificent panorama of . . . snow-capped peaks."[48] Yet overhanging the optimism loomed the real struggles that marked living in such a place. Clearing slides, repairing snowsheds, and bringing in shovel gangs had become a way of life; and avalanches, intense snowstorms, and work-related accidents punctuated the mundane duties that characterized working for the CPR. The railroad annually employed five rotary plow crews and at least 150 snow removers for the Mountain Division—the section of track that ran from Laggan (now Lake Louise) to Revelstoke; and no matter how many sheds the CPR built, the slides continued to come down on the rails.[49]

In late February 1910, a terrific snowstorm struck the Selkirks. One seasoned CPR foreman remembered it as the worst storm he had ever seen. It lasted for ten days, alternating between snow and rain. During that time the railroad men worked nonstop clearing slides and digging out trains.[50] Many agreed that they had never seen a storm dump so much snow or last for so long. At least "seven feet had fallen in nine days . . . !"[51] As the storm raged throughout the Pacific Northwest, Revelstoke's newspaper readers empathized with an avalanche disaster near Wallace, Idaho, on March 2. A giant slide had swept over Mace, a mining camp of nearly 150 people. Fire bells alerted volunteers in Wallace to gather and take a special train to the site of the catastrophe, where they dug in the hopes of finding survivors—an emergency response familiar to the residents of Revelstoke. They read, too, of a second slide sweeping down, hitting Burke, the camp next to Mace. It seemed likely that the second avalanche had caught several of the volunteers.[52] In addition, rumors flew in Revelstoke about an avalanche on the GN line in Washington's Cascade Range, and later news confirmed that two GN trains had been "smashed to bits" at Wellington, that "few escaped," and all that remained was a scene of "wholesale destruction."[53]

Soon, however, a local horror would overwhelm Revelstoke. Just after midnight, "all of the Bells and Whistles in the Upper Town started to sound."[54] Two Revelstoke youths, Scott Calder and Charles Procunier, walking home from a party rushed to the firehall to find out what had happened. Along with 150 others, mostly off-duty CPR employees, they heard that a slide had buried several snow-clearing crews below Avalanche Mountain near Rogers Pass. Miraculously, the passenger train nearby, with four hundred aboard, was unscathed.[55] The volunteers grabbed shovels and rushed to a train called into disaster service waiting to take them to the site of the slide. Just after 1:00 in the morning the rescue train pulled out of the station.[56]

Of the fifty-eight railroad men buried in the slide, the only survivor was Bill LaChance, a fireman on a helper engine.[57] His crew was one of the few that still lived at Rogers Pass. He later described how on the evening of March 4, management sent them to take a rotary plow up to a slide that had covered the track earlier in the day. The evening's slide had come down, filling a cut plowed through about fourteen feet of snow, and filled it with snow and snapped timber. They picked up more crews along the way, including forty Japanese immigrants who were employed as shovelers. LaChance's crew "bucked" the slide with their plow until they reached broken trees. Then the shovelers jumped into the cut to break up and shovel out the pieces of wood. The foreman, Johnny Anderson, went to the nearby watchman's hut to telephone down to Revelstoke that the line would open soon.

Back at the slide, the scene of regular work changed in an instant. LaChance remembered that a wall of snow seemed to come out of nowhere, hurling his body out of the train. Wet snow filled his eyes and mouth and he "knew it was a snowslide right then. . . . It's a disgusting sight to see a slide, horrible," he recalled.[58] A strong wind seemed to pick up his body and toss it into the air. He covered his face with his hands as the slide tumbled him about, twisting and breaking his leg in the process. Finally he came to rest, and he clawed at the snow until he reached fresh air. Instead of the engine noise and shouting he expected to hear, everything lay eerily quiet under piles of snow. As he spit out blood and snow, LaChance called for help. Just when he began to despair, a brakeman's lantern broke the gloom. He called out, and the familiar face of Johnny Anderson appeared. In bewildered tones Anderson asked, "Bill, where are they all?" LaChance responded, "They're all gone."[59] Anderson gave LaChance his coat and headed back to the telephone to report the accident. Anderson called down to Glacier, the nearest stop, but his inability to explain what had happened—most likely due to shock—meant he had to make the four-mile trek through the snow to carry his message in person.

The slide brought out an unprecedented number of rescue workers. From the east 150 volunteers boarded a train from Calgary and headed to the site. In the meantime another huge slide came down on the tracks. No trains or people got caught, but the slide and continuing bad weather kept rescuers apprehensive. Tom Kilpatrick, superintendent of the Mountain Division, arrived and took over rescue and clean-up operations. As the days passed, more than 600 snow shovelers converged on the scene of the three slides, working to dig out the bodies and open the line.[60]

Those days took on a nightmarish hue as men faced the seemingly impossible task of finding the victims buried beneath the avalanche. The slide had broken all the trees in its path, creating a concrete-like mixture of snow, ice, and branches. In the wreckage, the bodies lay so tangled up that workers had to dig out the dead by hand.[61] The CPR officials organized the rescuers into small crews and fed them in shifts. The first bodies recovered were both burned and frozen: These men worked in the locomotive, and had been thrown against the train's firebox before suffocating and freezing under the snow. After several days, the CPR sent in paid shovelers to replace the volunteers.[62] Calder, the young man from Revelstoke, would always remember those horrendous days and nights as his transition to manhood.[63] When he volunteered to look for victims and risk his own life, he participated in the actions associated with older railway workers and became, in effect, one of the men for the first time in his young life—an important step as a resident of Avalanche Country.

EXPERIENCED WORKERS, RISK, AND DISASTER

Men in the Mountain West built confidence in their work practices over time, and this helps explain in part what motivated them to go to work under dangerous conditions. At the inquest that followed the tragedy in Revelstoke, bridge carpenter Duncan McRae, an employee of the CPR, explained that although the company paid men time and a half to dig out slides at night, the real reason men undertook the greater risk was because they "were only following out the custom of going out to do it. The men have never refused yet to go out."[64] McRae admitted that the crews would rather stay home during bad storms, "but it was the custom" to go even on the worst nights. He did not believe that the men thought they "would be fired if they refused." Rather, they accepted the extra risk as part of the job.[65] It remains unclear whether McRae was referring to both skilled and unskilled workers, but either way it is clear that he saw custom as the reason why men went to work when conditions were riskier than usual.

Other accounts at the inquest supported McRae's. According to road master Johnny Anderson, "It is not compulsory for men to go out at nights to clear slides and I don't know if men would be fired for refusing. I wouldn't fire them. A case of refusal has never been known."[66] Anderson pointed out that company policies included rules about shovel gangs' responsibility to clear the lines, but that as far as he knew the practice of working day or night, in spite of danger, had never come up as a point of contention among experienced trainmen, laborers, and management.

CPR engineer J. P. Ford also weighed in on the practice of the men working at night. "It has always been the custom" to do so, he said, and,

"There is no rule compelling a man to work at night but it is customary to do so."[67] Vic Anderson, another road master, reiterated the practice: "Men always go to slides day and night as a sense of honor and duty." He continued: "There is no rule forcing men to go out at night . . . [but] . . . I have never known of any case of refusing."[68] McRae and the others, all experienced trainmen, practiced the customs of their jobs and engaged in risky behavior out of a sense of obligation toward one another and responsibility toward their work. Even the coroner, Dr. Hamilton, insisted that the "unwritten custom among the men" of working at night dictated their behavior, and so the company could not be blamed for the fatalities.[69]

Rogers Pass survivor LaChance explained that he had no particular fear of another slide at the site because he did not think the location more or less dangerous than any other. He could not recall ever hearing of a slide in that exact spot—so although the accident he survived was unexpected, a second avalanche in the same spot seemed unimaginable. Although he recognized that working on the rails near Rogers Pass held an inherent danger, he felt secure as he went about his work because he believed that slides came down no more often there than in other areas. Predicting slides based on where they usually fell played an essential part in how workers evaluated risk. Furthermore, LaChance explained that he trusted his foreman, who held that position based on his experience working the Mountain Division. The foreman's responsibilities included deciding whether to post avalanche lookouts on especially bad nights; because no such precautions were taken, LaChance did not believe anyone expected the slide.[70]

Bridge carpenter McRae, who testified at the inquest that followed the Revelstoke slide, made statements similar to LaChance's. He admitted it had been a "bad night to work at a slide," but the "place was no more dangerous than any other."[71] In his recollection, no slide had ever come down in that spot. Furthermore, as the coroner concluded in his summation, the section of the pass held no special danger, and the "number of foreman killed showed it was unexpected."[72] The coroner's comment underscored that men with experience held knowledge about when and where slides happened, and if they did not expect one, then only an act of God could explain the event.

Custom sent men to work on stormy nights and influenced the decisions they made when work became tense because of weather conditions. Digging out a slide at night was inherently risky, but trainmen knew they could rely on their coworkers to be at their sides. This knowledge contributed to the special set of skills held by experienced trainmen. The combination of solidarity, knowledge, and bravado added to the trainmen's sense of obligation to their jobs and one another. These convictions help explain what took them back to work after tragedy befell their comrades. In Avalanche Country, work and environment became connected, and experience in their jobs provided mountain trainmen with specific knowledge that directly influenced the customs they developed. Rather than feeling alienated from nature, as some theorists argued was the case for workers in Industrial America at the time, these men had assimilated their environmental knowledge into their work practices.

TEMPORARY LABORERS CONSIDER RISK

Compared to their foremen who worked the Mountain Division sections, the majority of the temporary workforce hired in the winter, mainly as snow shovelers, did not have a detailed knowledge of the environment. Their approach to acceptable risk stemmed more from how much the company paid and the treatment they received than it did from their experiences or feelings of duty and custom. As a result, the dynamic that existed among CPR management, rotary crews, foremen, and shovelers further complicated encounters in Avalanche Country. The inquests that followed the 1910 slide in Revelstoke presented the opinion of veteran railroaders, such as LaChance and Anderson; but of the fifty-eight men killed on March 4 in Revelstoke, thirty-two of the forty-two shovelers were workers brought from Japan by a labor supply company that contracted with the railroad.[73] Seasonal laborers rarely left behind written records, but their actions with respect to difficult working conditions and disasters reveal a good deal about how they balanced risks against their paychecks.

Many immigrants who came to work in mines, at lumber camps, and on the railroads had no mountain experience at all. A few from certain parts of Japan or the Alps might have knowledge of slides, however, the case of one shoveler, James Moffatt from Ireland, was more typical.[74] After he and a few friends spent all the money they had earned at a lumber camp on a spree in Vancouver, the young men signed on as snow shovelers in D. J. McDonald's gang in Revelstoke. Less than a week later he died in the 1910 slide. Moffatt's mother, Anne, wrote to Superintendent Kilpatrick to explain that her son had left Ireland to earn money to send home. James had supported his "delicate father," and without his contributions the family was in dire straits. [75]

Young Moffatt's questionable ability as a breadwinner aside, his brief stint on the railroad indicated that he had little experience predicting or understanding slides. Nor, would it seem, would he have had time to develop a sense of duty to his employers. Moffatt's safety, whether he recognized it or not, depended on the more experienced men who oversaw the gangs. In fact, it seems entirely possible that men like Moffatt had no idea of the risks they took when they signed on as shovelers and might only realize it after their arrival on the scene or in the split second before the wall of snow crushed out their lives.

Asian laborers, most without mountain experience, also came to the Canadian West to make money. Little is known about the Japanese workers who died at Rogers Pass, but a letter written after the slide by Mehar Singh, an Asian Indian gang leader, gives some idea of what their work experience might have been like.[76] Although the Revelstoke newspaper declared that all of the dead deserved "full sympathy and love," foremen on the CPR sometimes treated their Asian laborers poorly. In a letter to Superintendent Kilpatrick, Singh, self-proclaimed "Hindoo Boss," listed a series of complaints against the CPR related to conditions on Rogers Pass. Singh told Kilpatrick that his gang had "been working heartly [sic] whether it was day or night, whether we were hungry or thirsty, thinking that it was bad time on the Company, and it was bad time on us too."[77] Through six nights without blankets and the constant threat of more slides, they continued to shovel.[77] Singh reminded Kilpatrick that the GN had offered the shovelers $1.75 a day to dig out their tracks, and the sawmills paid $2.00 a day. Even then, his gang did not quit because "if we will quit the job the Company will think that the Hindoos are no good."[79] Two other Asian gangs quit anyway, clarifying that the risk versus reward on the line hung in the balance for immigrant workers.

Singh had experience working for the CPR and with Road Master Johnny Anderson, but Anderson resigned after the slide in response to losing his brother and friends in the disaster. Singh found the behavior of the new road master unacceptable. He "abuse[s] us all the time," he reported, and he grabbed the men by the "neck and shoulder, and gives us push and kicks us with his legs." The Italian shovelers, he argued, were being treated better than the Indians, adding insult to injury. As a result, several men had quit, and the rest of the men could barely take the treatment. In his several years in service to the CPR Singh had "never Saw Such treatment by the Road master towards the boys." He asked that Kilpatrick reassign his gang to another division or else send them back to Vancouver. He concluded with a note about his good service: "In the times of the Slide I supplied 26 men to the Company."[80] Singh expected the CPR to reward his men's commitment to clearing the line. In this way, he also reminded Kilpatrick that the shovelers, while more easily replaced than the skilled workers, remained essential to rail operations when disaster struck.

When shovelers walked off the job or complained about how the company and their bosses treated them, they contested their subordinate position and challenged the complicated and hierarchical relationships that underlay working for the railroad. The shovelers assessed risk, reward, and disaster with a different set of understandings and priorities than the experienced men of the company. A far cry from the harmony and purpose suggested by the sensational coverage of railway workers and slides found in magazines and newspaper, or even the custom of working at night as explained by the experienced trainmen, unskilled laborers had a different calculus.

COMMUNITY RESPONSE AND QUESTIONS OF RESPONSIBILITY

In Revelstoke, the skilled railway men had developed strategies that justified their dangerous work and that to some measure mitigated the risks they took. These men also existed within a larger community, a town that consisted of families and service industry operators living in diverse neighborhoods inhabited by both skilled and unskilled workers. These individuals and groups found different meanings and had different ideas about who was to blame for the 1910 slide.

The news had barely spread about the slide when people in Revelstoke began to discuss how the tragedy could have happened. Those first on the scene, like Scott Calder, who claimed the horrors he saw aged him overnight, were changed by the experience. Others, who had lost a husband, brother, or son, felt the crushing numbness and bewilderment that comes with tragedy. Almost immediately two competing narratives emerged. One story told of the heroic efforts of the CPR men felled in the line of duty. The other declared that the slide did not represent an "accident" at all, but instead was the result of the negligent attitude of the CPR toward its employees. Regardless of what position they took, people wanted an explanation for what had led to the deaths of so many men.

Carefully worded articles in Revelstoke's *Mail-Herald* emphasized that the men had died fulfilling the "duty of their calling," but the paper also speculated about problems with the new track recently built by the CPR at Rogers Pass to reduce the grade.[81] Whereas a snowshed had covered the old track, the new track, which paralleled the old, had no protective covering. The company had decided that the new track did not need a snowshed because no slides had occurred there in many years, reinforcing the accepted wisdom of experienced men who said history was the best predictor of where slides would happen. In its defense, the CPR believed the site a safe zone. The company line was that families should blame the unusual storm for the disaster, not the CPR. The CPR also traded on its safety record to support its position that it had not acted negligently.[82]

But the newspapers wanted to know if the CPR should have taken precautions, such as building a snowshed over the new track. The subsequent answers contributed to the mounting evidence that the railway had not taken proper safety measures before the catastrophe. Was it possible that the railway men had anticipated the slide? Some who worked that night claimed they expected the slide that "usually comes down in that vicinity" at any time. In fact the men had worked on in spite of the "crash and boom" of slides farther off on the mountainsides.[83] The heavy rains, they speculated, on top of the snow created perfect conditions for slides. But an even stronger indictment of the CPR in the newspaper account stated: "It may be said the present conditions are exceptional, but we understand from the railway men, who know what they are talking about, that these slides are getting worse every year, and will continue to do so." This was because "the forests, which formerly protected a great part of the road, but were destroyed by fire during and since construction, rot away, thus giving clear sweep to slides from the deep snow banks which cover the mountains in winter."[84] This set of facts contradicted earlier statements given to the paper that no slides had been known in that area for a long time, challenging the railroads' assertions that it was believed to be a "safe zone."[85]

In an effort to control the story and absolve the railway of responsibility, president of the CPR, Sir Thomas Shaughnessy, issued a statement to the press on March 7. The slide happened due to "unprecedented conditions," he explained.[86] The unusual circumstances of a "heavy fall of snow" followed by "rain and warm weather" had created the unstable snow conditions that resulted in the worst accident ever suffered by the CPR.[87] Shaughnessy made two important points, reminding the public of the CPR's safety record and emphasizing the role nature had played in the tragedy. Blame lay with the storm, he said, not the CPR.

The CPR found some allies in the press. Regional papers, such as the *Calgary Daily Herald*, worked to protect the company's reputation. Even as it printed the long list of the dead, correspondents reminded readers that all transcontinental routes battled snow and avalanches in the mountains, and the CPR had a better record than most.[88] The blame for the tragedy resided not with the organization but with the ferocity of the storm, writers reported, and the CPR had met the horror of the accident with acts that were "equal to the occasion."[89] One writer declared that two slides in one place proved an event "exceptional in mountain philosophy," so rare that the accident was "altogether unexpected."[90] This tantalizing reference to "mountain philosophy" supports further speculation that mountain people's knowledge of their environment gave them insight into the nature of slides. Even as the paper soothed the fears of future passengers and those who shipped cargo on the line, their assurances were undermined by reports on avalanches that continued to come down the tracks on Field and along the Kicking Horse River.[91] The newspapers, like the CPR, smoothed over the contradiction between claiming that the train could operate without incident in the mountains and then blaming a storm for the disaster. While the CPR tried to escape responsibility by calling the event an act of God, it also tried to inspire confidence in its ability to take passengers and freight through the mountains safely.

But as shock settled into mourning, and as the community members of Revelstoke tried to make sense of the avalanche on the pass, they framed the tragedy from their position as railroad employees or as friends and relatives of CPR men. The dangers of working for the railroad had helped create a worker culture that balanced the risks of the job with the safety yielded by experience and a language of obligation that rewarded the reputation of men who willingly undertook these dangerous jobs.[92] But the customs that led experienced men to work did not justify the massive loss of life, nor did they lessen the problems for those far away, like Moffatt's mother, who plaintively wrote to the superintendent: "I am not able to work now as my heart is broke about my Dear Son cut away. Just in the bud of manhood away where I will never see his grave."[93] She pleaded for monetary compensation to alleviate the pain of his death. Although Kilpatrick saw to it that Moffatt received a decent burial and that his family received the money from the $100 life insurance policy he had taken out when he was hired to cut timber, the company did not help the family beyond that.[94]

Like the experienced workers' ideas about when and where slides happened, many community members based their reactions on their own experiences and their opinions of the company. The company was hypocritical, they concluded, as they considered the difference between the CPR's actions and its words. Although the company made all efforts to reopen the line, suggesting humans could win the battle against the snow, they claimed that deadly avalanches were an inevitable act of God. Residents also resisted the palliatives of a local clergyman who explained that "it has been God's will to call them to him, and we must accept it believing that it is for the best, though our earthly sorrow be great."[95] But for many, God's will was an inadequate answer to why the avalanche took down so many men. The terrible reality of so many lives lost brought into focus the limited utility of the language of duty and obligation and an act of God as sufficient explanation.

Public displays of grief engulfed the community in the weeks following the slide. The mayor proclaimed a "half holiday," and citizens poured into the streets to display their sorrow and support the grieving families. Many attended the funerals of James Moffatt, Vic Carlson, and James Gullach at Selkirk Hall, and even more "with bared heads in mute sympathy for the dead" stood along the town's streets to watch the funeral procession, which included religious and fraternal affiliates, CPR employees, hearses, and conveyances for female mourners.[96] A few days later, the town held a memorial service at the opera house to honor all of the men who died in the slide. The elaborate service included several addresses from religious leaders and prominent citizens and musical performances that praised the men "overwhelmed while on duty."[97] The names of the dead were listed on the service's program, divided by European and Asian ancestry.[98]

The local paper called them "true heroes" who had died "in the faithful performance of personal duty. All were heroes because they fought well for their families and those dependent on them."[99] If any lesson had to be learned from this event, it "was to rise above the forces of nature, to build better railways, to plan better and to design their undertakings on a higher and better plane."[100] It urged the mourners to think of the tragedy as a call to continue man's battle against nature, and it reinforced the idea that a man's financial support of his family was a virtue that counterbalanced dangerous work. These pronouncements spoke both to the bravery and skill of the railroad men and to their efforts to control the natural world. E. M. Cook, who lived in Revelstoke and worked for the CPR, repeated these themes when he spoke to the sorrowful crowd. There was nothing like working on the railroad to reinforce the "uncertainty of life," he said, but the death of men on the rail lines "was the toll that it cost them to enjoy the advantages of modern improvements." In exchange for the loss of men "in the discharge of their duties on the railroad . . . was its [the disaster's] value in developing the sympathy of their fellows."[101] He hoped the tragedy would pull the community closer together. In Revelstoke, these sentiments elevated the attributes that made living in Avalanche Country bearable, but these kinds of pronouncements served the CPR's agenda as well.

The slide at Rogers Pass affected everyone in Revelstoke. By giving victims a proper send-off, community members acknowledged the friends, family members, and strangers who risked their lives daily on the railway. Whereas the volunteers who worked to uncover victims represented the immediate community response, the funerals embodied the community's use of their institutions, including unions, churches, and philanthropic organizations, which existed to assist townspeople in a place where few government regulations protected workers.[102] Furthermore, funerals as rituals marked the loss of loved ones and helped community members repair the disruption caused by the avalanche.

Throughout the Mountain West winter problems continually impeded production and transportation. These problems accentuated the contradiction between companies' actions to protect their property from avalanches and their assertions that avalanches represented chaotic nature or acts of God. Whether perceived as wild or predictable, the environment remained central to mountain workers' experiences and influenced the development of their communities. Railroad workers developed complicated strategies to cope with the risks they faced at their job and used the knowledge they possessed to predict slides to reinforce the pride they took in their work and to establish a hierarchy within the workplace that made newcomers dependent on those with more experience. The system worked to reduce risk, but it also made the chances taken a badge of honor within avalanche communities.

Furthermore, experienced workers and temporary employees responded to danger differently. The problems faced and decisions made by Singh and the other Asian Indians emphasized how workers accepted risk based on a number of factors and how they calculated whether to stay on the job based on their assessment of the situation. Their balance of risk and reward weighed treatment by the boss against the danger of the work and wages received. The fact that seasonal laborers sometimes walked off the job when conditions became bad enough suggested that they accepted the risks of the job less willingly than their more experienced counterparts.

Community members also evaluated the risks taken by the railroad men and became an important part of disaster response when they participated in rescue efforts, cared for the bodies, and participated in funerals. They worked out issues of blame by discussing their reactions, reading newspaper accounts, participating in inquests, and accepting relief payments. Furthermore, they would contribute to the memory of the disasters as they told stories about them as the years passed, building collective knowledge about the risks and responsibilities of living in Avalanche Country.

FIVE

WHO'S TO BLAME?

> It was . . . alleged that the section house was built near the base of a high and steep mountain, and in a place subject to snowslides, and dangerous on that account; that the company was aware of said danger; that the plaintiff and her children had never before resided in a region of country subject to snow-slides, and had no knowledge of snowslides . . . and that the company did not at any time notify or apprise the plaintiff or her children of the danger.
>
> —*The Supreme Court Reporter*, 1893

N 1893, CHRISTOPHER A. PILGRIM SUED HIS EMPLOYER, THE DEN-ver & Rio Grande Railway Company (D&RG), asking that the company take monetary responsibility for the injuries he received when a snow-slide hit the train he worked on as a porter. He filed his case in district court in Arapahoe County, Colorado, and won. But in an appeal by the company, the Colorado Supreme Court overturned his case, ruling that the railway could not have predicted the slide. The court deemed the incident an act of God and absolved the railway of any responsibility for Pilgrim's medical issues.[1] Unlike the court, Pilgrim believed slides probable enough in Avalanche Country that the D&RG should have protected him better or taken responsibility for his injuries. Like other trainmen in Colorado and their counterparts in Washington and British Columbia, he was convinced that slides held predictable characteristics, believed his employer had acted in disregard of these characteristics, and so sought compensation for his injuries based on this conviction. He believed that his employers had a responsibility to either protect him or compensate him if hurt by a slide at work—a danger that they should have expected.

The same slide led to another suit, this time by passenger Jennie A. Andrews. She claimed the D&RG should compensate her for injuries incurred. Like Pilgrim, she won her case in a lower court from a jury of her peers. But the D&RG appealed to the state court, and again the judges overturned the jurors' decision, delivering an act-of-God ruling. As recorded in the court report: "An inevitable accident or act of God, does not give rise to a cause of action."[2] Andrews, like Pilgrim, wanted the railway company held accountable for her injuries but found out that her conceptions of responsibility and blame did not match the company's or the court's.

The question of whether people could predict slides or whether they were acts of God complicated cases that dealt with the relationships between workers and owners in industrial settings, as did incidents on mass transportation that affected passengers. Around the turn of the last century, the creation of state railroad commissions that investigated railway accidents signaled an acceptance of the inadequacy of older methods of determining the causes of accidents and assigning blame, but case law still favored corporations over individuals. Although more juries were finding in favor of plaintiffs against companies and had begun awarding larger damages for those injured on the job—a "small revolution" in terms of pointing "the finger of blame at employers"—appeals courts' rulings often overturned jurors' decisions. Higher courts' resistance to changing common-law doctrine was especially obvious in cases in which acts of God came into play.[3] Pressure also came from companies that sought to escape responsibility from damages; they depended on act-of-God rulings to eliminate criminal prosecution for negligence and relied on plaintiffs' difficulty in providing sufficient burden of proof in civil suits to escape moral and financial repercussions.[4]

The courtrooms, where victims sought justice, served as a public forum where employees, employers, passengers, and other stakeholders aired their opinions about the predictability of slides. Testimony highlighted the importance of local knowledge to those who lived as everyday participants in Avalanche Country, as well as how that knowledge affected those who passed through the mountains. Reactions to catastrophes became increasingly complex because of the growing number of those affected who all had their own notions of acceptable risk and ideas about who or what to blame when tragedy struck; snowslides, as noted, could be seen as unknowable acts of God or as predictable and avoidable tragedies.

Disasters in Avalanche Country accentuated the continued importance of expertise for safety; disasters also thrust the shortcomings of liability law in the Progressive Era into the spotlight. Moreover, disasters brought people and nature together in unsettling ways that undermined confidence in industrial-age technology and man's mastery of his environment. Inquest and courtroom testimony offer richly textured arguments from both sides of the debate about avalanches as acts of God. Of course, court records cannot be taken entirely at face value, because they represent a highly structured venue. Nevertheless, how locals understood their environment and the range of ideas regarding responsibility for disasters come through loud and clear.

MARCELLA DOYLE

At 6:00 PM on March 10, 1884, a huge snowslide ran full tilt into Woodstock, a station stop a few miles below the DSP&P line's Alpine Tunnel. The avalanche slammed into the section house, telegraph office, water tank, boarding house, saloon, and various other structures. Of the nineteen people caught in the slide, only one man worked his way free. He staggered to Pitkin, ten miles away, for help.

News of the disaster flashed across the telegraph lines, and railroad superintendent Smith sent twenty-five men from the Alpine Tunnel crew down to the site. Meanwhile, thirty citizens of Pitkin volunteered to search for those buried. The rescue crew immediately set out on skis. After forty-eight hours the two parties had recovered ten cadavers and found five survivors. On the night of March 12, exhausted diggers called off the search and began their grim journey back to Pitkin. The skiers strapped the bodies on sleighs, and it took them nearly all day to haul their burdens over deep snows that constantly upset the sleds.[5] Several days later they recovered two more bodies. The last corpse lay entombed until spring.[6] The five who lived included two women, Marcella Doyle, who was buried for two hours, and Celia Dillon, buried for three and a half hours.[7] Ironically, materials designated to build a snowshed composed some of the avalanche debris, suggesting that the company was well aware of slide danger in that place.[8]

Doyle ran the section house owned by the DSP&P where railway employees took their meals. The widow and her eight children had gone to live there in November 1883. Her daughters helped at the boarding house. Her sons worked for the railroad.[9] Six of her children, who ranged in age from ten to twenty-three, died in the slide. Dillon, the other female survivor, had been engaged to Martin, the oldest Doyle son.[10]

Rather than seeing the tragedy as an act of God and retreating into mourning, Doyle held the DSP&P responsible for the deaths of her children. She brought two actions against the DSP&P, a subsidiary of the Union Pacific Railway, in the Eighth Circuit Court. The first suit addressed personal injuries. The second asked for compensation for the wages lost to the family by her children's deaths. She sought $5,000 for each dead child and $20,000 for injuries, damages, and loss of property.[11]

Lawsuits like Doyle's offer concrete examples of the intricacies of liability law in the late nineteenth century. In cases that sought to prove company liability, it was the plaintiff's job to establish company negligence. Also, the relationship between the plaintiff and defendant held an important role.[12] Doyle, because she decided to make her case as an employee of the railroad, would run into multiple problems because of legal precedents based on three principles of common-law doctrine, by and large borrowed from the British. The first principle, assumed risk, dictated that employees should have understood the danger of their jobs when they signed on, thereby absolving the employer from compensating a person hurt or killed at work. This theory extended to payments to the families. The second principle, contributory negligence, held that an employer owed nothing to an employee if that worker in any way caused the injury. The third principle, fellow servant, absolved a company from responsibility if another employee caused the accident that led to an injury. All three of these principles favored the employers. They also implied that employees had a clear understanding of the risks associated with their jobs. Doyle's pursuit of a case against the DSP&P came at a turning point in civil suits involving corporate liability. On the eve of a period when laws would begin to codify workers' compensation in ways more suited to the hazards of the Industrial Age, Doyle had to contend with weighty legal traditions that did not adequately address the dangers of industrial work.[13]

So what if an employer withheld information that put an employee at risk? This was at the heart of Doyle's case: The railway failed to provide her with adequate information about the dangers of where she worked. Her lawyers argued on her behalf that Doyle had little mountain experience and knew nothing about slides and that the railway had a responsibility to inform her of these risks. Because it failed to do so, it should be held accountable for the death and damage caused by the slide. In this case, if a jury could be convinced that the railway knew about the danger of avalanches in Woodstock and had put Doyle and her unwitting family in danger, the company should pay.

To show the railroad's negligence, Doyle had to present a very convincing case that proved the railway knew about the dangers of the location and had failed to inform her. According to this line of argument, the lack of information nullified assumed risk on Doyle's part and made the company liable. Doyle explained that when she began work at the section house, the railroad knew of the danger of the area but never told her or her children about it. She stated that avalanche scars marked the mountainsides above the section house. These scars proved to anyone familiar with slides of the danger of the site. But the Doyle family had no such expertise, and therefore they should have been warned before deciding to move into the company's building. This particular knowledge, apparently withheld by the railway, indicated that Doyle thought those with mountain experience knew how to predict slides. Furthermore, she argued that a rocky protrusion above the building obstructed the view up the mountain. This meant that the danger remained obscured even to someone experienced in gauging the likelihood of avalanches. Lacking both experience and a clear view, the Doyles remained ignorant of their dangerous situation. The railway, with knowledge of both, became doubly culpable for the tragedy. It is important to note that this question of the predictability of slides would vex both sides of the case.

As the testimony unfolded it became clear that experienced mountain residents believed that history predicted slides best. According to the plaintiff's witnesses, the railroad must have remembered a slide that ran within two hundred feet of the section house in February 1883, proving the danger of the location. In fact, they continued, at the time the railroad built the line through Woodstock, a civil engineer working for the railroad had warned the superintendent that the section house sat in a dangerous spot. Such reoccurrences of a slide at one location almost guaranteed more would follow. Therefore, the argument went, the railroad had prior knowledge of the danger of slides in the area and should take responsibility for the death of the children. Because the railroad failed to give Doyle information about slides in the area, it had denied her the right to choose whether to live in such a deadly location. Clearly, the lawyers concluded, the company was liable.[14]

The railroad, however, recounted a different view of the events. Testimony in the company's favor began as follows: "Snow-slides do not always follow beaten tracks made by former snow-slides on the same mountain side, but frequently depart therefrom."[15] The railway's lawyers argued that the 1883 slide, rather than following a straight path, divided into several smaller slides, one hitting the section house. The defendant's lawyers argued that in no way could the railroad have predicted this would happen or that a similar split would happen again. Furthermore, they argued, it snowed much more during the winter of 1883 to 1884 than it had the previous winter, rendering predictions even more difficult. From March 1 to 10, it snowed continually, and the tracks had become hopelessly blocked with drifting snow. The railway admitted that marks of earlier avalanches existed on the mountainside above the section house, but it believed the building sat in a safe site. The company based this opinion in part on the slide of 1883, which covered the tracks and had shut the train down for the remainder of the winter but did not threaten the structure in question. It also noted that the avalanche in 1883 had tumbled down in a different spot than the one in 1884 and had caused little damage. In addition, the warning to the superintendent about slides on that section referred not to the section house but to a spot a mile farther up the track. More to the point, the railroad argued that slides held both expectable and random characteristics—a stance that gave them leeway to vouch for the reliability of their service and to defend themselves against damages when predictions failed.

The defendant's lawyers went on to provide more detailed information about why the company believed the section house was in a safe location. The railroad's representatives argued that the rocky prominence, which Doyle said blocked her view, actually acted as protection from slides. Further, buying into the wisdom that trees held snow in place and that lack of trees marked known slide paths, the broken pieces of large trees in the slide debris proved that no slide had come that way in many years. Yet according to one Pitkin resident who testified, the slide resulted from the removal of timber from the mountainside. In the process of building the line, workers had cut down most of the trees for ties and building materials. He claimed that without trees to hold the snow, slides became even more likely.[16]

Finally, the company lawyers explained that Doyle did not work directly for the railroad because her income came from the payment for meals she prepared for railroad workers. Instead, they argued, she was a tenant of the company, an entirely different relationship. This made any arguments about assumed risk moot. A landlord's duties toward a tenant ended once the lessee chose to move into a location, under the premise of *caveat emptor*, or let the buyer beware. Once a tenant moved into the house the landlord had no further responsibility to warn the tenant of impending dangers. Its only responsibility rested with an inherent failure of the structure itself. So, the defendant's lawyers claimed, "in the absence of fraud, misrepresentation or deceit, a landlord is not responsible for injuries to his tenant by reason of a snow-slide or avalanche."[17] This assertion meant that unless the railroad had intentionally deceived Doyle about the possibility of slides before she moved in, it had no responsibility for the damages incurred.

After both sides rested, the judge instructed the jurors on their duty. He reminded them of the defendant's argument that the railroad did not directly hire Doyle or pay her wages. The law, he instructed, did not allow them to assign blame to the landlord in such a case. In effect the judge told the jury that they had to find for the defendant. They complied with the judge's instructions, and Doyle lost her suit in November 1886. Dismayed by the verdict, Doyle appealed her case to the U.S. Supreme Court. Her lawyers charged that the lower-court judge had wrongly pressured the jury to find in favor of the railroad. The Supreme Court's decision to review the case indicated the importance of the liability questions related to disasters, employees, tenants, and of course judges' instructions in these matters. Although technically the matter at hand was whether the judge had rightly instructed the jury, the predictability of slides in Avalanche Country came under consideration as well.

In January 1893, nearly a decade after Doyle lost her children, the justices began to review her case. Their primary task lay in deciding whether the circuit court judge had put undue influence on the jurors or instead had correctly pointed out what the law required. Thus the nature of the relationship between Doyle and the DSP&P would determine the validity of her suit. Even if the justices decided that Doyle worked for the DSP&P, tort law resisted changes to precedents that concluded employers were not liable for injuries that happened at work, peripheral to the work itself.[18] Given the nature of common law in the 1880s and 1890s, it seemed unlikely the justices would overturn Doyle's case. Interestingly, rather than focusing only on Doyle's relationship to the DSP&P, they also chose to discuss whether or not slides represented acts of God or foreseeable disasters and whether some mountain people had knowledge that allowed them to understand the nature of slides. Ultimately, that discussion would play into the justices' final decision.

First, the justices established the exact nature of the relationship between Doyle and the DSP&P. They found that she made her living off of the payments made to her by the railway employees who ate at the boarding house, rather than from the railroad. Even though the railroad sometimes garnished the wages of their employees to pay Doyle what they owed her, this "did not convert Mrs. Doyle into a servant of the company or change her relation to the company as a tenant at will of the company's house."[19] The Court concluded that the company did not pay Doyle, and therefore it did not employ her directly. The relationship between Doyle and the DSP&P was that of landlord and tenant, not employee and employer.

Even so, the Court examined other questions relevant to the case before making its final decision. Again, the fact that the justices did not immediately dismiss the case at this juncture pointed to the importance of the questions at hand. Avalanche cases were not the issue per se but rather a reexamination of matters related to landlord responsibility and natural disasters. Avalanches did not happen everywhere, but hurricanes, tornadoes, earthquakes, fires, and floods came into consideration frequently in the courts, and the justices used the Doyle case to clarify the level of responsibility of landlords for injuries caused by such disasters. For example, did the company have prior knowledge of the danger of the building site? If so, did it then have a duty to inform the tenant of the possibility of a slide? Here, the Court drew from established matters of landlord liability to reach their opinion.

At this time, few tenant rights existed, as the rule of *caveat emptor* suggested. Prior court rulings, however, informed the justices' analysis. For instance, in the case of *Bowe v. Hunking,* the Court had ruled that a landlord held no greater responsibility for injuries caused to people who lived in a building at the will of the lessee, such as a tenant's children, than to the tenant herself.[20] The Court further cited the case of *Woods v. Naumkeag Steam Cotton Co.* to illustrate their point.[21] In *Woods,* a tenant's wife slipped and fell on icy steps. The plaintiff argued that the landlord, having prior knowledge that the steps tended to accumulate ice and snow, should have constructed railings. The Court decided, however, that as the tenant had seen the steps before moving in, and because the steps had not changed in between that time and the accident, the landlord had not misled the tenant about the staircase. Nothing required the landlord to alter the steps for the tenant or anyone he brought to live with him, in this case his wife, and so the Court found in favor of the company. Another point of case law referred to was *Laidlaw v. Organ.*[22] This case boiled down to the question of a seller's obligation to inform a buyer about "extrinsic circumstances, which might influence the price, though it were exclusively in his possession."[23] The seller, or lessee, they decided, had "no moral or legal obligation" to inform a buyer or tenant, if the buyer or tenant could have obtained the same information through asking questions. This, of course, put the burden of knowing what questions to ask on the potential tenant, and the assumption that he or she would know what to ask in the first place. Doyle's argument was that she could not have known what to ask as she had never before lived in Avalanche Country, therefore the company had more responsibility than usual. The justices, however, did not see the circumstances as unusual enough to negate the precedent, and thus applied it to the question of the railroad's duty to inform Doyle of any avalanche danger in Woodstock. If Doyle could obtain the information on her own, the company had no duty to educate her. Thus, the responsibility of learning about the risks of living in Avalanche Country fell on the tenant, or Doyle in this case. Her children, whom she brought to live with her, assumed the same risks she did, and the railway had no duty to warn them of any dangers that Doyle could have found out about on her own.

Each case referenced revealed the difficulty in proving liability. When the Court decided that the relationship between Doyle and the railroad fit that of tenant and landlord, her chances of recovery dwindled. The relationship of tenant and landlord held different legal ramifications than that of direct employee. The only responsibility a landlord had to the tenant existed in the condition of the building itself at the time the tenant agreed to move in, not any catastrophe that befell it. Because the railroad had not misrepresented the solidity of their building, and because the structure did not cause the slide, under the law the railroad held no responsibility for the building's destruction and the deaths.

That decided, the final aspect of the case turned on perceptions of slides near Woodstock. The Court declared the "plaintiff's evidence failed wholly to show that there was any special and secret danger from snow-slides, which was known only to the railway company, and which could not have been ascertained by the plaintiff."[24] In addition, the justices determined that the section house sat in no more or less dangerous a location than any other building built on a mountainside in a place that accumulated deep snows. Any danger of slides was incident to the region and should have been as apparent to the plaintiff as the defendant. This determination overlooked the fact that while slides fell often in the mountains, many people did not see where or when they fell as random.

After reviewing all the records, the Supreme Court concluded that the circuit court judge had advised the jury correctly, and therefore the jury's decision in the lower court was sound. The justices exonerated the railroad of "any positive act of negligence" and of the charges that it had acted fraudulently by failing to mention the danger of snowslides in the area. They dismissed the two writs of error that made up the case—the first because it sought restitution for Doyle as an employee of the railroad. Because the Court had determined Doyle was a tenant, her case rested on unstable ground from the beginning. The justices' opinion asserted, "It has often been held by this court that it is not a reversible error in the judge to express his own opinion of the facts, if the rules of law are correctly laid down, and if the jury are given to understand that they are not bound by such opinion."[25] This meant that the judge's comments were allowable as long as the jurors understood that they could act independently of his suggestions. Second, as the Court had opined from the beginning, "the law does not imply any warranty on the part of the landlord that the house is reasonably fit for occupation," nor does it "imply a warranty that no accident should befall the tenant from external forces, such as storms, tornadoes, earthquakes or snow-slides."[26] Doyle's case could go no further. The defeat of her appeals contributed to the body of case law that denied tenant safety and absolved companies of responsibility in the event of a natural disaster. This case also devalued knowledge about the predictability of avalanches and became part of the legal record, which would make it more difficult for future victims to recover compensation.

Doyle's efforts to use the courts to hold the DSP&P accountable revealed her hopes to force greater responsibility from employers (and landlords). Furthermore, this case, and likely Doyle herself, argued that the disaster that struck her family was not "natural" at all. Doyle worked with railroad employees with more experience in the mountains than she had. Most likely she had heard from them that people could predict slides, and this knowledge informed her perspective on the tragedy. Notions of risk and responsibility came into play when Doyle fought to define avalanches as a disaster that the railroad could predict and tried to use the legal system to assign blame.

On the other hand, to the railroad's advantage, the circuit court and the Supreme Court chose to see the tragedy as an act of God. This view of disasters, which defined the events as outside of human control, absolved the company of any wrongdoing and protected the company from future lawsuits. The cases examined by the justices demonstrated Doyle's slim chance of payment from the DSP&P. They also revealed the difficulty of proving a natural disaster such as an avalanche could happen because of negligence. There is an argument to be made that there is often nothing "natural" about natural disasters at all, and that those exposed to the greatest dangers often have little power over the decisions that expose them to risks. Destructive floods, for instance, often affect the socially and economically disenfranchised more because projects like levees are built to protect the wealthy but not the poor from high water. Socioeconomic and racial bias also influence who suffers the most when disaster strikes. Marginalized people often live in more vulnerable housing and often do not receive the same services following a disaster, and similarly do not have the advantage of financial safety nets, like insurance. Doyle, a poor, uneducated woman, seems a perfect case study to support these kinds of arguments. Unfortunately for Doyle, however, she did not have access to modern historical and sociological interpretations that might have given empirical and theoretical support to her quest for justice.[27] Instead, because cases like *Bowe v. Hunking* established that no special protection applied to those who lived with the tenant, Doyle had no legal claim to compensation.[28] This meant the railroad did not owe Doyle for the loss of her children's lives or wages, as she alone had invited them to live with her. She alone bore the legal responsibility for their living at the section house and for any "acts of God" that descended on her unsuspecting family.

COMPANY RESPONSE IN REVELSTOKE

In Revelstoke, too, questions of responsibility followed the 1910 slide, as seen in the flurry of letters and telegrams sent back and forth between Canadian Pacific Railway (CPR) management, victims' families, and their lawyers in response. On April 26, William I. Briggs, Revelstoke barrister, solicitor, and notary public, wrote to Mountain Division Superintendent Tom Kilpatrick asking if the CPR intended to make payments to the families of those who lost their lives on Rogers Pass. The lawyer had several clients interested in filing claims, but he thought there existed a "chance of amicable settlement." Briggs wondered about the company's "attitude" on this matter.[29] Two days later Kilpatrick evaded response by telling Briggs he could not move forward with the inquiry until he (Kilpatrick) had the names of the people involved.[30]

But other letters written between CPR officials in response to inquiries from victims' families or lawyers elucidated the "attitude" taken by the company. General claims agent W. H. D'Arcy wrote to Superintendent Kilpatrick on July 25 about J. McLennan, a bridgeman who died in the slide. McLennan's executor had written to D'Arcy, who handled all the financial inquiries related to the slide, asking that the CPR make a settlement to McLennan's mother. D'Arcy expressed surprise to Kilpatrick that the solicitor, J. B. McKenzie, was pursuing the case, as he had spoken to him in Revelstoke and made very clear that "the Company disclaims liability in these cases, and there is no use in the parties expecting the Company to deal with their claims on basis of legal liability" because the inquest findings gave them some protection.[31] The CPR resolved several claims, but only after the lawyers acknowledged the "defence[sic] of 'vis major' (superior or irresistible force of nature)."[32] This protected the CPR from any further suits from those parties. Furthermore, the CPR made sure that the recipients accepted the money on the terms that it represented relief rather than compensation. D'Arcy dealt with several potential cases with relief payments, and eventually paid Mrs. McLennan $500.[33] When other families threatened to sue the CPR, they challenged the inquest's findings. Their attempts to force more responsibility from the company spoke to their financial desires but also indicated that enough evidence existed to support those claims. The CPR answered these difficulties by supplying "relief" payments, payments that did not carry the legal stigma attached to settlements.

Kilpatrick did not openly disagree with company policy. He did show, however, that he found it somewhat troubling when he wrote to General Superintendent F. F. Busteed on December 9, stating that he wished to give $14.50 in donations for the families of victims to McLennan's mother as she "was only paid $500 by the Claims Agent."[34] Kilpatrick also personally handled several insurance claims, including that of James Moffatt, who had taken out a $100 life insurance policy when he went to work for a timber company, before coming to the railroad.[35] But the sympathetic (and business-minded) attitude taken by Superintendent Kilpatrick did little to influence greater company policy toward those who lost loved ones.[36] Yet even as the CPR scrupulously paid back wages, tracked down insurance payments, and assisted with funeral expenses up to $85, it denied that the company held any direct responsibility for the deaths and relied on legal protection that defined slides as mysterious acts of God.

Too, the CPR dealt with its skilled and unskilled workers differently. In a letter written by Superintendent Kilpatrick to General Superintendent

Busteed, Kilpatrick urged Busteed to "deal liberally with the dependents of employees[,] as work of handling rotary plows on stormy nights is always more or less dangerous and when a plow is working it is impossible to hear any slides running." Moreover, Kilpatrick saw the advantage of the work customs of the men and wanted those customs that kept men on the job even during the worst storms to stay intact. As such he hoped Busteed would see the advantage in compensating the families because "it would create a good feeling amongst our men." This, he thought, would help the men go back to work, safe in the knowledge that the company "will provide for their families." He mentioned no such consideration for the shovelers, their lack of skills making them replaceable. This refusal to pay compensation extended to the Japanese shovelers. In their case the CPR went even further, arguing that because the Japanese were contracted laborers, the company had no direct financial responsibility for dealing with the bodies. They assigned all funeral expenses over to the workers' direct employer, the Nippon Supply Company.[37]

Through its actions, the CPR contributed to the growing complexity of encounters in Avalanche Country that came with industrialization. First, the presence of the company gave employees or families another entity to blame besides individual actions or an act of God. Second, the company itself became involved in defining the meaning of disaster and had a vested interest in calling it an act of God rather than a predictable accident. In addition, it had considerable power to shape public opinion through its spokespeople and the media. Third, liability law favored the company's position. By persuading victims' kin to take "relief" payments, it escaped problematic lawsuits from those families in the future. This of course did not eliminate the fact that many families and injured employees blamed the company for their pain and suffering.[38]

In Canada, the absence of a civil suit following the Rogers Pass slide leaves many questions about how a local jury might have decided a case, but the actions of a handful of Revelstoke's citizens hint that some disputed the definition of the disaster as an act of God. The first inquest jury, after hours of deliberation, ended up deadlocked over the question of the company's contribution to the cause of death. Coroner Hamilton had to convene a second inquest to come back with a verdict of accidental death for all the victims.[39] The inability of the first jury to agree reinforces the conclusion that many mountain people agreed that slides had predictable characteristics and blamed the company for the deaths. But the second inquest's finding meant no criminal charges could be filed against the CPR. The Revelstoke inquest was representative of most inquests that followed deadly avalanches.

Act-of-God rulings protected companies from criminal prosecution—and legal definitions of disaster supported corporate positions of innocence in civil cases—but victims still sometimes chose to use the courts in spite of the odds against them. Doyle's tragedy was uniquely horrific in terms of loss, and where her survival reinforced the importance of community rescues, her decision to pursue the issue of blame in the courtroom tested the law's power to assign blame in the event of a natural disaster and the extent of landlord or employer liability tied to such events. As a relative newcomer to the mountains, Doyle had confidence that those with more experience than she held important knowledge about the endemic dangers of the terrain. Her belief that locals could determine where slides happened informed her ideas about risk, responsibility, and blame.

At the same time, her case connected avalanches to wider legal interpretations of so-called natural disasters as acts of God. Doyle's tragedy and the subsequent suit she filed against the DSP&P showed that although community responses and networks of aid composed a crucial component of mountain living, they did not satisfy the needs of survivors in the aftermath of slides. Survivors rejected the idea that no one was to blame, and they wanted restitution. The testimony of the victims and railway workers provided striking evidence about the nature of slides and why even with expanding notions of corporate responsibility in the Progressive Era avalanche disasters evaded easy conclusions about who was to blame.

SIX

DISASTER IN THE CASCADES

If we get a chinook wind, the whole town of Wellington is going to hell.
—Basil Sherlock, 1910

O N FEBRUARY 22, 1910, SARAH JANE COVINGTON, AGE 69, BOARDED
Great Northern (GN) Train 25 in Spokane, Washington. As she settled
in for the trip to Seattle she probably thought little about the partic-
ularities that allowed a train to climb through the Cascade Range. She
might have caught a glimpse of the train's engineer, firemen, or brakemen
and considered the nature of their work for a moment. But like most passengers, she expected an uneventful journey. The clanking wheels and
bursts of steam from the engine promised that the train could make the
trip easily. Yet the sights and sounds of departure hid the complex work-
ings of man and machine that made rail travel possible. The operation of
the trains depended on a human workforce under constant pressure to
make choices when technological difficulties or other problems arose during the journey. The safety of their coworkers and the passengers, like Covington, depended on those decisions.

Covington began keeping a journal the next day when the train was
delayed on the east side of Cascade Tunnel on February 23.[1] She wrote that
she found the mountains lovely and her rail car cozy as she settled in for
the wait. By the next day, as the snow continued to fall, her mood worsened
as she heard rumors that the food supply at the cook shack was getting low.
Other passengers, too, had a growing sense of isolation, as the mounds of
snow grew higher around the train. Word that the telegraph wires were
down also worried passengers, who had been using the line to send messages to loved ones about their predicament. That night spirits surely lifted
when their train was moved through the tunnel and parked on the other
side at Wellington, on a passing track off the main line.

On the passing track, or siding, as the trainmen called it, the passengers found themselves stalled again, along with a mail train also delayed by the storm. Anxiety rose when news came the next morning that a slide had destroyed the cook shack on the east side of the tunnel and killed two workers there. In fact, the word was that the slide had come down right where their train had been. This certainly added to the growing impatience of passengers, and it also contributed to an apprehensive atmosphere aboard the train. By that evening the situation had worsened to the point that some male passengers called a meeting that led to a petition for action. Covington, on the other hand, busied herself with her reading and disdained the other entertainments available to the passengers, such as smoking, card playing, and drinking.

By Sunday, February 27, Covington's morale had sunk further. While she tried to keep busy soothing some other female passengers, she commented on her anxiety and "growing sense of fear and loneliness."[2] She envied the women who had their children with them to keep them company. She further worried over the choice that some men were making to leave the train and hike out—an option she did not have available to her, because she was physically unable to make such a journey. By Monday the combination of fear and tedium drove Covington to help another passenger, Anna Gray, sew clothes for her baby. By this point the trains sat buried in the snowdrifts, and the snow on the peaks above the train seemed to hang precariously in place. Covington wondered if they would be stuck until spring. She turned to prayer and God's protection for succor. Other passengers worried that an avalanche would be the end of them all.[3]

The evening of February 28, the passengers and train employees had a party that raised the mood considerably. Most were soundly asleep when the avalanche came early on March 1. It slammed into the passenger and mail trains, pushing both into a ravine. A week after her trip began, Covington and ninety-five others lay dead in a gully, covered by snow and twisted metal.

SURVIVORS RESPOND

Of the ninety-six who died in the Wellington slide, thirty-four were passengers: four children, eight women, and twenty-two men.[4] Five other passengers were injured. Before the deadly slide, thirteen passengers—all men—had hiked down to safety. At the inquest that followed the disaster, survivors told about their ordeal. Edward W. Bowles was one of the lucky ones. On February 28, he and a group of men from the trains went to take a look at the slides west of the siding and ended up making it the few miles to the town of Scenic. When Bowles recalled the days leading up to his decision to leave the train, he did not remember his fellow passengers expressing any fear of slides, but rather recalled that they were complaining about the length of the blockade and wondering when it would end. Bowles, who left a brother behind on the train and then lost him to the slide, stated, "I was not much afeared," and it seemed to him that the railroad men had done everything in their power, working "day and night" to alleviate the situation.[5] Passenger John W. Merritt, who walked away from the train on Sunday, February 27, wanted nothing to do with the passengers' complaints—intimating that there were many. When asked if he thought the chance of slides in that place great, he answered, "I have not had experience enough in the mountains to see what other persons might," asserting his belief that only experienced men could make that call.[6] Nor did Merritt blame the superintendent of the Mountain Division, James H. O'Neill, or the other railroad men for the tragedy. He thought they had done all they could in such a situation. But Bowles's and Merritt's statements did not necessarily represent the consensus, and others who told about the days leading up to the catastrophe explained events differently.

R. L. Forsyth, a lineman riding as a passenger on Train 25, slept on the train the night the slide descended. Forsyth remembered that the possibility of slides scared the passengers and that they asked conductor Joseph L. Pettit if he could move the train back into the tunnel. Pettit explained the safety and sanitary problems related to the tunnel and assured them of the safety of the train. Forsyth expressed that, having no experience in the mountains himself, he found the situation frightening. Yet it seemed to him that the railroad men had done all they could to free the trains. He took assurance from Pettit's words. As a railroad man, however, Forsyth would be familiar with other trainmen and railway culture that followed practices based on experience.[7]

But Henry H. White, a salesman from Seattle and one of the few passengers to survive, took a harder view. His version of the events made the GN look careless with respect to the passengers' feelings and safety. White explained that as the storm continued and the days passed the passengers became more and more anxious. Especially after they heard about the slide at Cascade Tunnel that killed the men at the cook shack, the women grew progressively more agitated. Most of the passengers thought the trainmen should move the train either closer to or into the tunnel. White remembered that it was on February 25 that the passengers held their first meeting to discuss their options. The passengers had heard rumors about their deteriorating situation from various railroad employees and decided that they needed to talk to someone in authority, specifically Superintendent O'Neill. But O'Neill, who had gone down to Scenic, never came. On February 28, thirty-four passengers signed a petition that demanded O'Neill present himself to the passengers. Instead, Earl Longcoy, O'Neill's private secretary, showed up saying he acted on behalf of Arthur Blackburn, who was next in command to O'Neill. White and the other passengers involved requested that the company supply men to break trail down to Scenic for the passengers who wished to leave. Longcoy explained that he did not have enough men. The passengers asked if the company could send up the laborers at Scenic, but Longcoy said he could not do it. Dissatisfied with Longcoy's answers, White demanded that he fetch Blackburn, someone with authority, to make a decision.

A little later Blackburn arrived and tried to soothe the passengers' anger and fears. He insisted that they remained safer on the train than if they attempted the trail. The shovelers at Scenic could not come up to Wellington to help because they had to stay below to help clear the line. Blackburn would not authorize the evacuation of the women and children because the trail presented too many hazards. He said, however, that the next morning he would do what he could to help any male passengers who chose to leave.

According to White, the passengers then asked if Blackburn could move the train into the tunnel. The trainman answered that the train did not have enough fuel to move to the tunnel, nor did he have enough manpower at Wellington to clear the tracks to the tunnel. White and the other dissenters found their situation so unacceptable that they considered wiring out for attention and rescue, but they could not because avalanches had taken out the telegraph wires. At the inquest, White blamed O'Neill directly for failing to address the passengers' fears and also for the GN's lack of preparedness. He thought the GN should have expected the slide and acted accordingly. He remained bitter about how the inexperienced people on the train had attempted to gain an expert's opinion about their situation, but to no avail.

So while the passengers traded gossip with railroad employees and each other, their fear of slides increased. White explained that as the women carried on "hysterically" the men sought answers to calm their anxieties. But by the time the passengers spoke with Blackburn the situation had gone too far. Snow had buried the trains, coal was low, there were not enough shovelers, and slides covered the tracks east and west of the siding.

Other factors compounded the tragedy. Several of the passengers planned to hike out the morning of March 1, but the slide intervened, taking all on the trains down the embankment. White asserted that at the time he personally did not fear a slide, putting his faith in the trainmen's experience. "I took it for granted," White said, "that those people knew more about it than I did."[8] In this way White echoed the sentiments of other survivors who assumed that the trainmen had their safety in mind and made decisions based on protecting the passengers. But in hindsight White judged their choices more critically: The disaster was clear evidence that something had gone horribly wrong. In his view, human error and complacency played a key role, and in retrospect White saw that a chain of errors led to the disaster, namely the shortage of coal, the position of the train on the siding, and especially the labor shortage that occurred after the shovelers at Wellington quit.

As in Revelstoke, local laborers were scarce in the Cascades, and recent immigrants, many Italian, usually filled the dangerous jobs. At Wellington, seventeen of those killed were identified as "laborers."[9] And like their counterparts in Revelstoke they sometimes protested their dangerous work and refused to risk their lives for low pay.[10] According to passenger White, when the train had first become trapped, shovelers had diligently worked "eight hours a day in snow up to their waists."[11] But as conditions worsened, they demanded fifty cents an hour, thirty cents an hour more, from Superintendent O'Neill. O'Neill recalled, "I told them twenty cents an hour and their board and they demanded fifty cents an hour and I told them we would not pay it and told them to get out."[12] They all walked off the site, an act that White asserted put the passengers in grave danger. Risk, as it turned out, had a price. In the Wellington slide, the unwillingness of one group to take on more risk without additional compensation possibly put others in greater danger, and some workers' actions were at odds with reported assertions of altruism and working-class solidarity.

Frederick G. Dorety, the GN's lawyer at the inquest, also questioned White closely about how he understood the role that O'Neill played in these events: Didn't he think O'Neill had done everything in his power to clear the tracks to get the train out of the mountains? White retorted that when the passengers sought someone with authority to reassure them, O'Neill was nowhere to be found. This, he thought, was a breach of the due care and sympathy the passengers deserved. When Dorety asked White if he thought the fact that the railroad men slept on the train with the passengers showed how safe everyone thought they were, White replied: "Yes and no; we also know that familiarity breeds contempt."[13] The trainmen, as White interpreted it, had developed an immunity to fear. They had become so accustomed to the danger of slides they did not necessarily notice the immediate peril and so failed the passengers. Even though the trainmen's testimony reveals no such contempt for slides, White would not be swayed in his opinion that the GN, and O'Neill in particular, should take responsibility for the deaths. He also painted a vivid portrait of the men gathered in consternation, seeking action, while the women stood by growing more upset by the hour, suggesting they all had a heightened fear of their situation and a growing sense that they were at great risk.[14]

Besides Covington's recovered journal and White's testimony, other survivors mentioned the general disquiet that pervaded the train. At the inquest, Lucius Anderson, a porter, recalled that many of the passengers seemed nervous. Passenger Lewis C. Jesseph, who walked out before the slide, also testified that he feared a slide, but his concerns abated when he heard Bailets the hotel keeper say that no slide had occurred where the train stood in his eighteen years living at Wellington. Still, Jesseph's restlessness motivated him to leave the train.

Passenger John F. Rogers explained his experience in more detail. It seemed to him "that everyone who was on the train was in a state of quandary. Their minds seemed bewitched, as was that in the legend of Sleepy Hollow. I know that I, myself, scarcely knew what to do."[15] Did Rogers think the other passengers felt as angry as Mr. White? Rogers did not know, but it seemed to him that the railroad men did all they could in the face of so much snow. On February 28, Rogers decided to hike to Scenic. He admitted that the reason he took the risky trek was because he worried that a slide could hit the train. He added that he would have taken any lady in his care "rather than stay in the mountains."[16] He saw it as up to each man to decide his actions, and he chose to walk down to Scenic. Rogers saw safety as an individual responsibility rather than the obligation of the company. Although none of the other passengers who walked out articulated it as clearly as Rogers, none who left the trains held the GN responsible for the tragedy the way White, who stayed, did. White put all the responsibility on the superintendent and the company, whereas those who left the train and took action for their own safety seemed less inclined to blame the GN. White instead framed the tragedy as a failure of leadership and an indictment of the customs that governed running trains through the mountains.

Passengers on the train at Wellington did not experience the days leading up to the tragedy or view the disaster itself identically; for Rogers and White the actions of the trainmen factored into their recollections of the event. Rogers believed they had done all they could—but White did not. Both men recounted the mood on the train with enough similarities that it seems clear that the passengers were alert to the danger of slides and grew increasingly alarmed as the days progressed. Their fear of potential slides more than implied that the potential risks at Wellington were understood not only by those who worked the Mountain Division but also by those who found themselves unwilling captives below the precipitous slopes.

In addition, passengers' perceptions of the responsibilities of the trainmen came not only from the heightened anxiety found on the train due to the terrible conditions but also from the larger range of expectations they had regarding due care when they boarded a train. Due care, an aspect of the law pertinent to passengers on common carriers, is the legal doctrine that holds it is the responsibility of the carrier to pick up passengers (or freight) and deliver them safely and on time to their destination. By and large, the testimony of railroad men not affiliated with the GN at the inquest found that the GN, O'Neill, and the employees' actions met the requirements of due care and followed practices customary to other mountain lines. Passenger safety came first, but that certainly did not mean doing what the passengers requested. Trains could not be run based on passengers' fancies, because "they are not practical people in that line of business particularly."[17] So according to the reckoning of the trainmen themselves, even if passengers *felt* neglected and scared and did not want to be on the siding, they certainly did not have the knowledge to gauge risk, the experience required to make good decisions, or even the judgment to question the choices made by the experienced men.

EMPLOYEES RESPOND

As White's assertions suggested, the decisions made by the trainmen came under scrutiny following the Wellington slide. Testimony at the inquest and a subsequent lawsuit revealed that custom, similar to the practices followed in Revelstoke, had dictated action on those terrible nights. At the trial *Topping v. Great Northern Railway*, a suit filed by the son of a victim, lawyers asked why the train had been left on the siding below the hill, on a track that allowed trains to pull over so that others could pass, rather than moved into the nearby tunnel.[18] Mountain Division Superintendent O'Neill explained at the inquest and trial that he never once considered moving the trains into the tunnel for protection. The dangers inside the tunnel—such as the potential build up of gases or a collision with incoming plows—far outweighed any chance of slides above the siding.[19] Although there was a system that let oncoming trains know if a train already occupied the tunnel, making it theoretically safe for one train to stay in the tunnel, O'Neill explained that he had expected the rotaries to need the tunnel as they passed back and forth over the tracks.[20] Moreover, he never suggested that the train be moved even if conditions worsened because no precedent existed for leaving trains in tunnels. The previously mentioned risks of fumes, collisions, or getting stuck were just too high, in O'Neill's opinion.[21]

Others also testified that moving the train into the tunnel would go against longtime practices. Traveling engineer J. J. Mackey, with ten years on the Mountain Division, confirmed that in the interest of safety, the siding made the most sense. He even went so far as to claim that if his family had been at Wellington, he would have had them sleeping on the train located on the siding and definitely not in the tunnel. Locomotive engineer J. C. Wright, a fourteen-year veteran in the mountains, commented: "All our experience and all our knowledge of those things we gain by something which has happened before."[22] The men had taken action based on lessons learned over time.

Experience and safety concerns precluded leaving trains in tunnels and also influenced ideas about how to avoid avalanches. Trainmen believed that sites where no slide had happened before were safest. This meant that where there had been no prior slide activity, the men would conclude that the conditions did not warrant a breach of protocol. After the fact, they knew that the snow above the siding had been unstable, but before the slide in question they would have expected trouble nearer the tunnel—a known slide path. Wright could not emphasize enough that "men learn by precedent" and that those lessons directed their actions at Wellington.[23] It appeared to Wright that no matter where they put the train, "It would have been criticized as an error in judgment" if a slide hit it.[24] He concluded that any official who put the train in the tunnel "would have been criticized from one end to the other."[25] The customs that governed the trainmen's actions meant they did not question O'Neill's orders about keeping the passenger train on the siding.

Again and again, the question of whether the siding presented a "safe" site arose. At the Wellington inquest, Pat Ryan, a laborer with eighteen years' experience in the mountains, acknowledged that slides could strike anywhere at any time, but by and large, knowing where slides had happened before served as an important guideline that improved safety. Robert Swartz, a trapper who sometimes worked for the railroad, added that his experiences had taught him "that where a slide has come once, that there is liable to be another slide afterwards."[26] When J. E. Campbell, trainmaster for the Northern Pacific, Seattle Division, gave his inquest testimony following the Wellington slide, he declared that in his experience a slide happening where none had occurred in twenty years represented an "exception to the rule."[27] If they had suspected the train was in peril they would not have allowed it to stay on the siding. W. R. Smith, the Cascade Division superintendent for the GN, would later explain that when he had lived at Wellington from 1898 to 1902, he had never seen or expected a slide where the March 1 avalanche fell. When conditions turned threatening, Smith and his family had depended on their understanding of how to determine "safe places" and retreated to snowsheds and sites where slides had never happened before. As he put it, "We would consider a place safe where in our history there hadn't a slide come theretofore."[28] When trying to determine why the tragedy occurred, the number of dead forced those involved to examine the decisions made and their system of predicting slides. The trainmen agreed that history had proved a reliable method— although not on this occasion.

Like people who lived in mountain mining towns, the railway men argued that other factors could contribute to the likelihood of a slide occurring. Logging, and fires that denuded hillsides, aggravated avalanche danger. Logic dictated that trees on hillsides acted as defenses against slides, as well as proof that no avalanches had descended in a place in a long time. It made sense for the lawyers who defended the Denver, South Park, and Pacific Railway Company (DSP&P) against Marcella Doyle to argue that broken pieces of large trees in the slide debris proved that no slide had come that way in many years, just as it made sense for the witness for the plaintiff to point out that deforestation made slides more likely. Determining how many trees existed before a slide fell depended on witnesses, who often failed to agree; nevertheless, most concurred that the amount of timber on a hillside mattered.

In Wellington, the relationship between slides and bare slopes came under scrutiny. Some questioned whether recent forest fires had denuded the slope. But Mackey testified that the amount of timber on the hillside seemed sufficient to keep the snow from sliding under normal circumstances. Key to understanding the Wellington disaster, he pointed out, was that abnormal conditions prevailed that week and that night. Therefore, even if the hillsides had less timber than in the years before, which he was unwilling to admit, he did not think this significant. In his opinion, once a slide of this unusual type started, trees, whether burned over or alive, could not stop it. Similarly, GN superintendent O'Neill testified that the slope above the siding was covered with dead timber and stumps.[29] In the three or four years that he had been in charge of that section he had never noticed a change in the amount of timber standing. Still other workers testified that the presence of trees and stumps on the slope had reinforced their reasons for trusting in the safety of the siding. Either way, they agreed that the presence or absence of trees on a slope could affect slides.

Assessments about where slides would happen also took into account the terrain. Trapper Robert Swartz, during his testimony at the inquest, reported that "a man can" determine where slides are most likely to occur, and they tend to descend "in the gulches."[30] Pat Ryan commented that when he looked at the hillsides he believed "she [a slide] would take that draw. There is a draw all around that hill. It would come pretty swift there."[31] Knowing the terrain, he believed that "no one ever expected that slide to come along that sidehill there."[32] William E. Flannery, the telegraph operator at Wellington, believed that slides were more likely to come down "perpendicular" hills rather than "sloping" hills like the one above the siding.[33] Mackey thought the train sat in a safe place and believed the GN men had acted appropriately given the situation.[34] These men were describing the characteristics of both loose-snow avalanches that followed gullies and ravines and slab avalanches that broke off along the top of a hill, usually with a convex shape. No gullies ran down to the siding, and the hillside above it did not have the characteristics the men associated with slab slides.

The assertions of experienced railway men, however, demonstrated how pervasive custom, rather than risk, was in guiding skilled workers' actions on the lines. Their testimony following the tragedy at Wellington highlighted their faith in judging the level of slide danger and why what happened that night went against their expectations. At the inquest that followed the catastrophe in Washington, Mackey declared that none of the trainmen feared an avalanche would hit the trains, because to their knowledge no avalanches had happened before at that exact location. Usually, Mackey explained, "the whole side of a mountain don't come down for half a mile or mile."[35] Another witness, Wright, agreed with Mackey. Slides, Wright remarked, "usually follow the same course other slides have—we have always found that up there."[36] Drawing on their expertise about the nature of slides, trainmen believed that those with experience understood the mountains best and so had made the right choices that week.

Yet, when Mackey stated the unusual nature of "the whole side of a mountain" coming down, he hinted at the bewilderment that many mountain workers felt when unexpected avalanches invaded their lives. Their conviction that they possessed an understanding of the nature of slides pushed them toward the conclusion that a series of unusual events or some anomaly of nature had caused the disasters, not some inherent flaw in their system. It becomes important to distinguish between the reasons why trainmen accepted some slides as acts of God and others as predictable and to recognize that the trainmen were neither pandering to their employers nor contradicting their larger view of nature when they did so. Rather, they were responding in ways connected to their environmental knowledge and their identities as mountain trainmen.

The experience that led skilled workers to believe in the predictability of most slides also led them to exclaim that these tragedies resulted from extraordinary, even unique circumstances. To make sense of these catastrophes, they reasoned that something extraordinary had happened. In Wellington, for example, many people believed that heavy snowfall and a freak electrical storm explained the catastrophe. Assistant trainmaster William Harrington, known as the "Snow King" because he managed the fleet of rotary plows, attributed the slide to a thunderstorm. In his mind, the likelihood of such a long snowstorm followed by an electrical storm happening again seemed highly unlikely.

Walter Vogle, the conductor of the mail train, Train 27, and Thomas McIntyre, an assistant road master with twenty-three years' experience, concurred that during their years in the mountains they had never seen a slide such as this one. It seemed to McIntyre that a combination of unusual circumstances must have started it.[37] And in Revelstoke, too, coroner Hamilton declared that the evidence led him to conclude that because no slides had happened in that exact spot in many years, the events of March 4 appeared unforeseen and therefore were purely accidental. As proof, Hamilton argued that the "number of foreman killed showed it was unexpected," presumably concluding that the experienced men would not have put themselves or their underlings at such risk.[38] The newspapers concurred. As previously noted, the Calgary paper had declared two slides in the same place on one night "exceptional in mountain philosophy."[39] These many statements, rather than leading the trainmen to doubt their belief they could predict slides, spoke to the surprise they felt when they did not—thus reinforcing their system in a roundabout way.

Others with experience in the mountains drew the same conclusions. W. R. Bailets, the hotel keeper at Wellington, theorized that rain created the conditions that led to the slide. As to the slide itself, Bailets stated that if anyone had told him how the slide happened, breaking along the top of the ridge rather than starting at a point and expanding as it went down, he "would have said 'No, that is not right.'"[40] Although his long time in Wellington led him to think that certain conditions could cause avalanches to happen almost anywhere, he maintained that he recognized a bizarre event when he saw one. He testified that he never expected such a large and horrible slide in that place. Superintendent O'Neill had also heard that an electrical storm had swept through Wellington that night. A storm, he thought, could explain such an unusually huge slab avalanche. Thus, according to O'Neill, only a series of unusual events could have led to the slide, in short making it an act of God.

Out of all the men interviewed, only Swartz admitted that the slide at Wellington shook his faith in his ability to predict slides. He admitted that after "this winter, I would not say that I can . . . tell where a slide would come from."[41] Even so, when asked if he thought the event would ever repeat itself, he answered, "Certainly not."[42]

Experience mattered most in all the decisions made at Wellington, according to E. W. Perley, a thirty-three-year veteran of railroad work and the railroad inspector for the state commission. Charged with checking on equipment and tracks to protect the traveling public and railroad employees, he testified that no trainman would leave a train in a tunnel or on the mainline unless forced to do so. In the three years he had held this position for the state, he understood "the custom has been on the Great Northern and all the other roads, to erect snowsheds where there has been a possibility of slides. . . . I do not think at Wellington, not having a slide in all these years, that a snowshed is necessary there."[43] He stated emphatically "the operation of a railroad through the mountain is governed by experience."[44] The railroad built snowsheds on that basis. In Perley's estimation, the situation was "beyond human ability to cope with," and he stated that he did "not see that anything could have been done more than has been done."[45] The state commissioner, the employees, and managers all agreed that experience had appropriately guided actions leading up to the slide.

All the testimony in this case indicates that mountain workers believed they could predict slides—and to a certain extent it appears that they could, given that tragedies of the magnitude seen at Wellington and Revelstoke had no precedent and were never seen again. This ability lessened the risks railway men took at work and provided a sense of greater safety. Knowing where slides typically occurred required years of experience in the mountains and contributed to decisions about where to build snowsheds and what places on the tracks constituted safe zones. Seasoned workers directly contributed to the safety of their coworkers by providing vital knowledge about what conditions led to snowslides, and they spoke assuredly about their understanding of the nature of slides and what increased the danger of an area, even after disasters occurred. When they considered the dangers they encountered, their knowledge played the most important role.

The Revelstoke and Wellington trainmen's reactions to these enormous tragedies, and their consistent and tireless support of the system of predicting slides, indicate more complex reasons than pressure from their bosses to motivate their testimony. The trainmen in Canada and the United States took great pride in their special skills, which countered job-related hazards and resisted interference in their workplace practices. Trainmen had diligently fought for union recognition, shorter hours, and higher pay (in fact, the switchmen on the GN had struck just a few months before the Wellington slide), and they countered environmental dangers such as avalanches through cooperation, experience, and a language of duty and obligation.[46] Their lives depended on a system they had developed over time and the possibility of a situation arising that was so dire that it would necessitate abandoning these practices seemed almost impossible. Nothing that had happened during the week before the slide at Wellington made the trainmen question their system or reconsider usual safety practices.

The number of employees who testified at the Wellington inquest confirmed the statements of Perley and others: From top to bottom and along all the different lines, trainmen relied on the methods developed by the Mountain Division community to reduce risk from avalanches.[47] It could be argued that job insecurity influenced the testimony of these trainmen, who wished to emphasize their special skills in the mountains. But a more compelling argument is that the trainmen's knowledge of nature, manifested in work customs and practices, led them to explain these particular disasters as somewhat extraordinary. To do otherwise would undermine years of experience.

THE VERDICT

After hearing the evidence, it took four days of deliberation before the inquest jury issued its verdict regarding the Wellington slide. The jury ultimately decided that the victims "came to their deaths on the 1st day of March, A.D. 1910, by reason of a snowslide at Wellington, King County, Washington, the cause of which was beyond human control."[48] It is worth noting that even when inquests returned act-of-God verdicts, they frequently made recommendations to improve safety. In Revelstoke, after the second inquest had "returned a verdict of 'Accidental Death,'" it "added a rider that the CPR should refrain from working its men in snowslides on stormy nights."[49] In Wellington, too, after the ruling, the jury added several admonitions. First, it found that the GN had not put the trains in the safest place. They determined that the spur closer to the tunnel sat in a less dangerous position. Second, the company did not have enough coal "to cope with all possible emergencies." Third, the evidence proved that thirty-five shovelers, who might have had an impact, quit due to O'Neill's refusal to increase their wages. Thus the GN had not acted consistently to ensure the "safety and welfare of the passengers."[50] These reprimands merely went on the record, however, and did not act as mandates for future actions.

Even though the inquest determined the GN was not criminally negligent, the company knew that claims and lawsuits would surely follow the decision. Hoping to fend off expensive lawsuits and more bad publicity about the slide, the company announced its intention to address any personal injury or death claims fairly and out of court.[51] Some families took payments: $1,000 to the families of married men killed and $500 to unmarried men's families. The GN strategically called these "gratuities or donations," to escape any sign of culpability.[52] Families that accepted these "donations" waived their rights to sue the company later. But $1,000 did not go very far for someone like the widow and five children left behind by conductor Joseph Pettit; she petitioned for more compensation, but met with little success.[53]

Not everyone accepted the "donations." Three years after the avalanche, the family of Edward Topping, a passenger killed in the slide, pursued a civil suit.[54] The case would have to prove that the GN could have, and should have, foreseen the avalanche at Wellington. It was no act of God, it claimed.

SEVEN

TOPPING V. GREAT NORTHERN RAILWAY COMPANY

> In order that a phenomenon should be an act of God it is not necessary that
> it be unique, that it should happen for the first time . . . it is enough if it is
> extraordinary, unprecedented and could not reasonably be anticipated.
>
> —Judge John E. Humphries, *Topping v. Great Northern*

I N FEBRUARY 1913, ATTORNEY FRED M. WILLIAMS FILED THE PAPER-
work that began a legal action against the Great Northern Railway Company (GN). William Topping, whose son had died in the Wellington
avalanche in 1910, hoped his lawyer could prove that his son, Edward W.
Topping, had died as a result of the "the negligence and carelessness" of the
company.[1] Any restitution would be used to help raise his grandson, Bill.
The GN had settled out of court several claims by passengers' families, but
likely in an effort to abort any more cases from going forward, it agreed
to go to trial with Topping in the hopes of proving the GN's blamelessness
once and for all.[2]

GN lawyer Frederick G. Dorety and his team organized to defend the
company. Using phrasing that deflected any hint of responsibility, Dorety
answered the suit with an affirmative defense. If Edward Topping had
lost his life on the GN train struck by a slide on March 1, he argued, then
"any damage sustained by the plaintiff, as set forth in said complaint, were
caused by *vis major* and by irresistible forces of nature beyond the control of this defendant."[3] The defense of *vis major*—a legal term meaning a
superior (natural) force led to the death—showed the company's determination to disclaim any responsibility for the disaster. Unless the Toppings'
lawyer could prove that the trainmen could have foreseen the avalanche,
the plaintiff did not have much of a chance, as tort precedents agreed that
negligence did not apply when deaths resulted from acts of God.[4]

Difficulties for the plaintiff began early in the case. Spokane County
superior court judge Henry L. Kennan denied Fred Williams's request for

documents held by the GN. Williams sought telegrams from Basil Sherlock, one of the telegraph operators at Wellington, which he had heard held incriminating evidence reading: "If we get a chinook wind, the whole town of Wellington is going to hell."[5] Williams also wanted any telegrams, documents, messages, writings, petitions, letters, memoranda, and so on in the possession of the GN relevant to the slide. Without the paper trail, Williams would have a harder time proving his client's claim that the company was aware of and concerned about the possibility of slides near the train.

The defendant gained another advantage with a change of venue. Dorety argued that holding the trial in Spokane hampered his abilities to present all the witnesses, who lived mostly in Seattle, Everett, and Wellington. With several other potential suits against the GN, Dorety proclaimed that his client needed to defend itself adequately. If the company lost against Topping, it stood to pay up to $90,000 to other potential litigants. Judge Kennan granted Dorety's request, and the trial went to Seattle, where King County superior court judge John E. Humphries would hear the case. Once the venue was established, Williams had to set up his case in Seattle, rather than from his home office in Spokane, and the defense had access to employees who had had several years to think about the events in question.[6]

Events brightened for the Toppings when their attorney's request to the court resulted in a motion to produce the passengers' petition for action to Superintendent James H. O'Neill, still held by the GN. The petition, signed by thirty-four passengers on February 28, requested a meeting with O'Neill to discuss immediate plans to evacuate the passengers caught on the train.[7] The motion also produced Topping's ticket stub, proof that he rode the ill-fated train. The court denied Williams's request for maps of the area and its snowsheds, documents that would indicate that the company understood the danger of slides and frequently took actions to mitigate their impact.

The GN brought nearly three times the number of witnesses to the stand as the Toppings, with the intent of bombarding the jury with evidence in its favor.[8] Losing the case would have implications for the GN beyond what it meant to the victims' families. Any successes against liability laws could undermine the protective cloak that judges had given to the GN and other railway companies and would contribute to shifting sentiment that railways should offer their employees and passengers more protection.

Beyond these legal implications, the battle brought into relief the contested meaning of disasters in Avalanche Country. Snowslides could not easily be categorized as acts of God because far too many mountain people had believed for thirty years or more that avalanches had predictable characteristics, as the Doyle case in Colorado proved. And the Toppings' lawyer would not make this a case about just the avalanche itself but rather about the actions taken by the GN that may have increased the likelihood of disaster. The conclusions drawn by those with mountain experience would become the deciding factor in the case.

Williams's strategy sought to demonstrate the many options the GN could have taken to avert a disaster, a disaster the company should have anticipated given its employees' experience. He hoped testimony from witnesses, passengers, and railwaymen would implicate the GN and confirm that its employees had been careless. Albert Hensel, a mail clerk on Train 27, testified that the mountainside above the stopped trains rose steeply and "had no timber"; he added that a flat spot nearer the tunnel had less of a hill above it, suggesting it as a safer location to leave the trains.[9] Henry White, the vitriolic passenger who accused GN Superintendent O'Neill of misconduct, recounted his conversation with trainmaster Arthur Blackburn and Blackburn's refusal to move the train into the tunnel or to help the women, children, and sick passengers leave the train. White believed that the GN's employees, including O'Neill, had been heedless of the passengers' needs and fears.

Williams called others to testify, too, including Coroner James C. Snyder, who had examined the accident site and presided over the inquest. Both Williams and Dorety focused on Snyder's observations of the topography and location of tracks and wreckage. Both were frustrated by his inability to explain the scene to their advantage, however, and he was excused. Susan Bailets, proprietor of Bailets Hotel on the pass, had lived in Wellington for eighteen years, and she declared that "snowslides are very frequent, but we could not tell where and when," offering something to both sides.[10] Williams used Bailets's testimony to demonstrate that the GN should have expected slides at any time; Dorety used it as evidence that this was exactly what made an avalanche an act of God.

Dorety worked the act-of-God defense into his cross-examination of Bailets, who admitted that until the Wellington slide occurred she had seen avalanches come down the gullies only. The old switchbacks, where the west portal of the tunnel now stood, she reported, always had the worst slides, and she supposed the hillside above the trains was less steep than in other places—assertions that ultimately aided the defense. Finally, Dorety asked Bailets, "How the length of the snow storm . . . compared with the length of previous long storms that you had known?" Her answer: "Well, it was much longer."[11]

Dorety's strategy focused on the unprecedented circumstances that led to the slide and the care taken by the railway to protect passengers. W. R. Smith, the Cascade Division superintendent for the GN, explained that the completion of the Cascade Tunnel in 1900 had eliminated 50 percent of the GN's trouble with slides on that route. The GN had taken precautions, he testified, to protect the tracks in years past. Smith told the jury that when he had lived at Wellington, from 1898 to 1902, he had never seen or expected a slide at the site of the March 1 avalanche. At times, however, he and his family had felt compelled to retreat to "safe places" such as snowsheds or sites at which no known slides had occurred. On cross-examination Smith clarified his point for Williams: "We would consider a place safe where in our history there hadn't a slide come theretofore."[12] If a slide occurred in a new place, then Smith said he would no longer consider it safe. Over the years, the railroad men had developed a catalogue of knowledge about where avalanches fell, although slides did occur in new places from time to time. Where Williams saw this as confirmation that the railroad men should expect the unexpected, the trainmen saw their system not as fool-proof but more than adequate protection for usual circumstances.

During cross-examination, GN employee John Calder's testimony took a turn that favored the plaintiff. He supported the defense's arguments that slides usually came down gullies, but he also added that a slide in 1903 had come down just west of the 1910 slide, "pretty near the end of the wreck-age." The 1903 slide, he said, had come down a hill not steeper than the one in 1910, but about the same grade. Calder's report implied that the possibility of a slide above the siding was not as far-fetched as the other witnesses had argued.[13]

Then Dorety questioned passenger George Loveberry to determine whether or not a passenger named Topping had discussed walking out to Scenic with the other men on the train. If so, he argued, Topping had broken his "contract" for safe passage with the GN, made when he bought the ticket. Williams objected, arguing that no other witness had testified to what the dead man had or had not done or said on the night in question. Topping had not left the train, and he had died in the wreck, and so, held Williams, there had been no breach between the passenger's expectations and the duty of the GN. The judge allowed Dorety to proceed, but Williams again objected to the question, and after a tedious afternoon of arguing case law, the judge ordered Dorety to withdraw the question.[14]

Even without Loveberry's final testimony, Dorety made a strong case. All of the GN's witnesses supported the company's position that there had been no way to predict this avalanche. They backed their claims with the knowledge and experience they possessed as seasoned Mountain Division employees. The GN had done all it could to clear the tracks, these witnesses argued, and the coal shortage had not impeded the clearing of the tracks or moving the trains. They testified that the switchmen's unresolved strike had not prolonged the blockade, and claimed that no one knew of a slide ever happening in that location. Furthermore, they noted that no fire had cleared the slope, making it more susceptible to slides.[15] The passenger witnesses chosen by Dorety confirmed that the trainmen had done all they could.

Ten days into the trial, Dorety and Williams concluded their questioning and made their closing statements. Judge Humphries issued twenty-five instructions to the jury. He explained that they needed to understand that the Toppings did not blame the GN for the avalanche per se but believed that the company had acted negligently when it left the train on the siding. The jurors had to determine if the GN was liable for letting the train get blockaded in the first place and whether the train's imprisonment resulted from a fuel or labor shortage. As the defendant denied all accusations of negligence, the burden of proof lay with the plaintiff's ability to connect Edward Topping's death to actions taken by the GN.

The judge explained that negligence came about with "the failure to observe for the protection or safety of the interests of another person, that degree of care, precaution and diligence which the circumstances justly demanded."[16] He reminded the jurors that although the law did not "make a carrier an insurer of the safety of its passengers," it did "require of such carrier the exercise of the highest degree of care, caution, foresight and skill for the safety of its passengers, compatible with the practical performance of the duty of transportation."[17] If the jurors concluded the GN had not acted in the safety and interest of the passengers, then they could find the defendant liable. If the GN had not taken "due care," if it had overlooked the potential danger posed by the hillside and if a safer place existed to put the train, they could find the company responsible. But if they agreed the event was an act of God—that is, the "snowslide was the sole cause of death, not contributed to or aided by any act of negligence of defendant"— then they must relieve the GN of any responsibility.[18]

"In order that a phenomenon should be an act of God," Humphries continued, "it is not necessary that it be unique, that it should happen for the first time." Instead, he argued, "it is enough if it is extraordinary, unprecedented and could not reasonably be anticipated, and in this case if the snow storm was extraordinary, unusual and unanticipated, and was the sole proximate cause of the death of deceased," then the accident was an act of God.[19] Because acts of God happened suddenly and unexpectedly, the jurors could not hold the GN accountable for a storm that put the train in the path due to chance. This statement suggested that if the avalanche had killed Topping, they could not find the GN liable, but the judge's earlier instructions muddled clear conclusions about the railroad's involvement in the disaster.

The decision depended on how the jurors chose to interpret the sequence of events. If they regarded the slide as a discrete event unrelated to the blockade the GN would owe Topping nothing. But if they chose to find that the events that led to the blockade and the choices made by GN employees put the train in its fated location they could find the GN at fault. The next day, Halloween 1913, Dorety filed a list of additional instructions that he wished the judge to issue to the jury. Not surprisingly, the eight points declared that the evidence presented did not support Topping's claims. The jury must not find the GN liable for Topping's death. But Judge Humphries chose to withhold these suggested instructions to the jury.

It took the jurors only one day to make a decision. On November 1, they found for the plaintiff and awarded William Topping $20,000. The same day, Dorety asked the court to overturn the decision in favor of the defendant, arguing that the evidence had not proven the defendant liable and that only an act of God could explain the events.[20] He also filed an alternative motion for a new trial, charging "irregularity in the proceedings," "misconduct of prevailing party and jury," "newly discovered evidence," "excessive damages," "insufficiency of evidence," and "error in law occurring at the trial."[21] In addition, Dorety filed exceptions to the court's instructions to the jury and to the judge's failure to read his additional instructions to the jury. On November 15, Judge Humphries overruled Dorety's motions, and he ordered that the GN pay William Topping $20,000 with interest from the date when the trial began.

Dorety immediately filed an appeal to the Washington State Supreme Court on December 6. As the lower court had reached its final judgment on the case, the GN had no choice but to go to the higher court or else accept a verdict that made the company vulnerable to more lawsuits, which would hurt not only its bottom line but also its reputation. Williams and Dorety spent the spring of 1914 writing briefs for the Washington state supreme court judges. The law left room for errors in judgment that could imperil passengers even when a so-called natural disaster occurred, yet as this case demonstrated, defining just how natural a disaster was could come under dispute. Ironically, both sides used the trainmen's method of predicting slides in their arguments—the elder Topping to claim that the GN knew to expect them and the GN to show that it did not.

WASHINGTON STATE SUPREME COURT

Unlike trial court, appellate court allowed both sides to offer prior case law in support of their assertions. Both legal teams approached their arguments by framing questions about how far common carrier responsibility could go, and when, if ever, the courts could deem a death caused by a natural disaster an act of negligence and therefore grounds for appeal. Dorety meticulously stated his rationale that the higher court should overturn the jury's decision. He framed the death of Topping within the context of the enormity of the storm. Slides had occurred elsewhere in the Pacific Northwest that week, in Mace and Burke, Idaho, and in Revelstoke, British Columbia. An expert government weather observer confirmed that the unusual number of slides in unexpected places proved the exceptional nature of the storm.

Numerous cases that ruled natural disasters acts of God served as precedents, including *Denver & Rio Grande Railway Co. v. Andrews* (1898), *Blythe v. Denver & Rio Grande Railway Co.* (1891), and *Denver & Rio Grande Railway Co. v. Pilgrim* (1897).[22] All three cases dealt with avalanches that struck trains in Colorado. Although cases decided in other states were not binding in Washington, they acted as guideposts where in-state precedent did not exist. In the first two cases, the Colorado supreme court had ruled "an inevitable accident, or an act of God, does not give rise to a cause of action."[23] A court cannot hold a company responsible for an avalanche that hurts or kills people when "it proceeds from causes over which the company has no control, and under circumstances which it is bound neither to anticipate nor to expect."[24] It followed from this premise that the court need only decide if the avalanche "was an inevitable accident."[25] Dorety argued just that.

In *Denver & Rio Grande Railway Co. v. Pilgrim* (1897), the Colorado supreme court overturned the jury's finding for the plaintiff because "a snowslide had never been known at that point before, nor has one ever been heard of since," and so the railroad could not have foreseen or protected the claimant.[26] The Colorado supreme court's decision took into consideration the methods for predicting slides and subsequently accepted these customs into case law, strengthening Dorety's claims. Dozens of other cases supported Dorety's position that carrier liability ended in the face of unknowable disaster: Courts across the nation had supported companies when they contended that snowstorms, avalanches, and cyclones had caused accidents. At the same time, this sort of testimony could potentially reinforce assertions that slides were predictable.

No matter the actions of the GN, Dorety asserted, "it is undeniable that the avalanche itself is an 'act of God,' and that for that, there is no human responsibility."[27] Multiple state supreme courts had ruled that when an act of God caused injury or death the burden of proof lay with the plaintiff to prove negligence.[28] The trainmen's methods for predicting slides were widespread and accepted enough that it seemed adequate justification for act-of-God rulings.

Dorety also objected to several of the judge's instructions to the jury. For instance, Judge Humphries had told the panel, "Before the defense of *vis major* can be available," the defendant must prove "it was the entire cause of the accident or injury, independent of any act of negligence on the part of the party pleading it as a defense."[29] This put the burden of proof on the defendant to show that the actual cause of the slide was an act of God wholly unrelated to the defendant's actions. According to Dorety this flew in the face of established case law. All three cases that arose from the Colorado slides, as well as other cases that dealt with natural disasters, held that "it is not negligent to run a train into a storm zone, knowing that a storm is prevailing."[30] Dorety forcefully concluded: "If there were any negligence, it was prior and disconnected, and not a proximate cause of the final damage."[31]

In fact, Dorety declared that the evidence proved that no negligence had occurred. As the company could not have foreseen the slide, did not cause the slide, and did not remove the timber from the mountainside, the court could not hold it liable. Previous cases made companies liable for negligence only when they were the proximate cause of the accident, and sending the trains through the mountains was too far removed from the accident itself, indicating prior negligence at worst. Yet, because the company could not predict all slides and never foresaw the trains' imprisonment, prior negligence did not exist, either. He emphasized that only those with experience and local knowledge of the mountains could properly judge a situation like that found in the mountains during that terrible week. Next, none of the controllable problems, such as fuel and labor shortages, actually caused the slide. The court, Dorety wrote, must overturn the jury's decision based on the insufficient evidence of negligence presented by the plaintiff.[32]

Fred Williams and L. F. Chester filed the "Brief of Respondent" on April 17, 1914. They contended that case law did not support the appellants as clearly as Dorety suggested. In Colorado the court had decided for the railroad, however, it stated in its opinion that it did not mean for the ruling to cover all circumstances surrounding slides. The court finding stipulated that subsequent courts could find a company liable if it did not take some precautions against avalanches. The court further concluded that the possibility existed that certain situations might demand that a company take "extraordinary precautions."[33] Williams also asked that the judges consider the cumulative nature of the danger at Wellington that made the event exceptional. Williams explained that "where the forces of nature have gathered gradually, obviously, uninterruptedly, carrying with them by necessary implication a warning of impending danger," the company had the responsibility to take action to protect its passengers.[34] Thus any claims by the defendant of a nonconcurrent act of God proved false when held up to the circumstances that led to the disaster. Without a doubt, Williams argued, the GN had to know a slide could happen at any moment.

Several facts, wrote Williams, supported his assertions of the concurring negligence of the GN. First, as the GN continued to build snowsheds along its line in response to slides, the increased number of sheds over the years proved that slides kept happening in new locations.[35] However, at the same time it also proved that slides recurred consistently in the same locations—or else the cost of building sheds would not be justified. The GN's new sheds demonstrated the company's awareness of the problem of slides and contradicted its testimony that slides usually did not happen in new places. Williams went further with this evidence and inferred that the addition of new sheds actually meant that, in the Cascades, "the occurrence of a slide at one place furnished no means of determining that a slide would not occur at another place."[36] He tried to convince the judges that people could not simply predict slides based on prior activity and so vigilance along the whole line was the only rational action. In fact a slide *"at the point in question was so highly probable that in all reason it should have been anticipated."*[37]

Dorety had found support for his position in the testimony of experienced railroad men, but so did Williams. The men expected slides to come down familiar routes, yet they also had admitted they had seen slides in new places every year along the mountain section. The experiences that taught them slides usually came down gullies also aided Williams's argument. Two gullies cut down the mountainside above the train, close enough that they should have caused concern. The judges must have been struck by how both sides used similar evidence but interpreted it to reach such vastly different conclusions.

Williams then tried to discredit the trainmen's experience, noting that if anything, their familiarity with slides should have led them to move the passengers out of harm's way. Again, case law reinforced his point. Poor decisions made by trainmen did not exonerate them from responsibility, but if they made the best decisions in a given situation they could not be held liable. Williams asked the judges to challenge the rules that governed the trainmen's behavior. Here, we are reminded of the words of passenger Henry White, who found the trainmen's attitude blasé in the face of danger, an outlook he attributed to the idea that "familiarity breeds contempt," or in this case an overly cavalier attitude to the perils at hand. White's account of nonchalant workers was influenced by the disastrous outcome of the journey—one can imagine he might have remembered events differently if all had survived the ordeal.

Although it appeared to White that the workers seemed careless of passenger safety, this interpretation does not fit with what we know about trainmen who worked the Mountain Division. Recollect that men went about their work even when the "crash and boom" of slides on the mountainsides rang in their ears.[38] They did not ignore the danger but rather accepted it as part of the work that they did and considered it part of their obligation as trainmen. Their duties also included following the practices developed over time in response to problems on the line. As a rule passenger trains did not wait on spurs because a spur had only one open end, making the train more likely to get trapped. The tunnel, a single track on the main line, presented an even worse choice for train placement, according to standard railway practices. In the same way, experience applied to how they understood snowslides. J. E. Campbell, trainmaster for the Northern Pacific, Seattle Division, stated that to his knowledge a slide happening where none had occurred in twenty years represented an "exception to the rule" that the railroad men followed. So "exceptional it would not lead you to expect another?" he was asked. He replied, "Certainly not."[39] One freak slide did not justify ejecting the customs and codes all trainmen in Avalanche Country depended on to mitigate risk. Campbell stood by the customs developed through experience and saw them as appropriate, not just in the Wellington incident but to running trains generally. More likely, the indifference White thought he saw was not a lack of concern about safety but instead an acceptance of danger. The trainmen knew that their lives hung in the balance but also considered that part of their work and took pride in the risks they undertook.

Williams argued that another act of negligence on the part of the GN included its unwillingness to retain its labor force at Wellington. If the GN had made an effort to keep the shovelers (i.e., give them the hazard pay they had demanded, to prevent them from walking off the job), they could have made sure the passenger train did not get stuck. Instead, O'Neill concentrated his efforts on freeing the rotaries and clearing the tracks at Scenic. In short, although the "immediate cause of the injury may be legally defined as an 'act of God,'" the facts at Wellington showed that the jury rightly held the GN liable and affixed an appropriate settlement.[40]

In their reply to the appellant brief Dorety and Brown made no effort to veil their contempt, writing: "If we are to be held at all in this action it must be upon this unsupported and illogical theory, of a city-bred attorney, struggling desperately to sustain a large verdict." The court, they insisted, must see the foolishness in accepting the interpretations of a "city" man with no mountain experience versus the facts presented by "men who have spent their lives in the mountains, and tested out these theories by actual observation of facts."[41] Dorety knew his strongest argument rested with the testimony of the experienced mountain men who knew about slides. Even if in this instance the "judgment of the experienced mountaineers proved wrong, and the teaching of past experience proved misleading," the storm that week was of such unusual duration and force across the whole Northwest, and the slide that broke off of such unusual size and shape, that it "vindicated" the "judgment of the experts to the effect that the only kind of slide they knew anything about, could not happen at that point." In fact, "it took something new in the line of snow destruction to prove that they were wrong."[42] The unusual nature of the slide explained why the men did not expect it. The argument that the slide was unexpected upheld the GN's defense and fit with the trainmen's testimony. Dorety hoped this would convince the judges to ignore Williams's attack on the trainmen. He concluded, "There was no cause for apprehending such a disaster" and so the judges must overturn the lower court's verdict.[43] No doubt he also hoped to assure future passengers and freight customers that the GN could deliver people and goods safely.

The court agreed with Dorety. On August 11, 1914, it reversed the verdict of the superior court. The two sides did not so much disagree on the facts of the case, the court found, as on how to interpret those facts. It seemed clear to the judges that an "unprecedented storm" contributed to the situation that led to the train's entrapment, but the respondent (Topping) failed to provide the burden of proof necessary to win the case.[44] As cases in other states had shown, when a train became delayed due to a blizzard, the storm is determined to be "an act of God," a finding that absolves "a common carrier from liability for loss of goods or for injuries to passengers caused thereby."[45] Here they cited *Denver and R. G. R. Co. v. Andrews.*[46] In this case the Colorado supreme court had decided that when a snowslide hit a train in a location where there was no history of an avalanche, and where there were no signs to indicate a slide would fall, it "was an inevitable accident, and that the carrier would not be liable for injuries to a passenger, caused thereby."[47] In addition, by law, the passenger assumed risk when he or she rode a train. The carrier's responsibility extended "only to such foresight and care as an ordinarily prudent person or company in the same business would use under all the circumstances of the case."[48] Following common work practices then, the trainmen took more than ordinary care when it came to protecting passengers from slides.

Next, the court determined that the appellant had successfully defended its position that when an act of God caused a death and the plaintiff accused the defendant of negligence, the plaintiff must prove "that such negligence cooperated with the act of God to cause the accident."[49] Unfortunately for Topping, the judges proclaimed, "This we are satisfied was not done."[50] The crews in Wellington had done all they could, according to the judges. The judges agreed with the appellant's use of the experienced railway men's testimony for predicting slides: Because slides usually came down gullies and because they knew of no slide in that location previously, the GN could not have anticipated the disaster. According to this argument, because the avalanche surprised even the most experienced mountain trainmen, no one could have foreseen the slide. The railroad men had used their experience to determine the safest place for the train, and thus no negligence occurred. Some "things are clearly beyond the knowledge of men."[51] This explained away, too, any question of moving the passengers from the train. As no trainmen saw the siding as unsafe, they did not act negligently in keeping the passengers on the train. The opinion concluded, "It is plain that this avalanche was what is known in law as an act of God," and as such the superior court judge should have either allowed for the nonsuit sought by the defendant or instructed the jury to exonerate the company.[52]

The clearest point of law amid the maze of liability issues was that acts of God absolved companies of liability. According to the Washington supreme court the jury charged with viewing the facts in the case erred in their verdict. The law stated that in cases in which an act of God, such as a snowslide, killed someone—as determined in this case by the inquest—no company or individual could be held liable.

Following the supreme court's decision, Williams and his team went to work drafting a petition for rehearing *en banc*, that is, in front of the whole court. They urged the court to consider "the importance of the questions involved therein, not only as they affect the material rights and interests of the Respondent, but because of their bearing upon the rights and interests of the general traveling public."[53] They argued that the judges needed to consider that their decision "will constitute a leading case wherein the doctrine, 'act of God' may be invoked as a defense by a carrier of passengers."[54] The court had to take into account the application of its decision to future cases. The importance of *Topping v. Great Northern* extended beyond the interests of the respondent. The final opinion would affect "the reciprocal rights and interests of carriers and passengers alike; and as a judicial determination of vital importance to all concerned it should reflect the combined analytical judgment of the entire membership of this Honorable Court."[55] It seemed to Williams that the court must have misunderstood the evidence in the case to reach the decision it did and that they had failed to take into account the value of this case to passenger safety.

The petition repeated the arguments made in the respondent's brief, noting that negligent acts of both "omission and of commission" made the railway liable, "notwithstanding the immediate cause was an 'act of God.' "[56] Williams, in a last attempt to change the court's decision, reworked the meaning of "experience." To rely on the judgment of experienced men for the safety of passengers presented a serious problem, because "it is common knowledge that constant contact with danger breeds for it, contempt; the habitué of danger becomes immune to fear or apprehension of the danger ordinary men readily observe."[57] This, he argued, validated the passengers' fears and made the trainmen's decision to sleep on the train suspect. Should the "measure of liability" in the state of Washington "depend on the" *ipse dixit* "of the railroad men," or should it be based "on all the facts and circumstances shown by the evidence?"[58] In other words, the railroad men's testimony had too many inherent biases.

Dorety and Brown then composed their reply. They supported the respondent's request for a rehearing *en banc* but hoped that the judges would uphold the earlier decision. They reexamined many points of the case and forcefully added that in storm after storm, year after year, the GN had a proven safety record. Never before had a slide killed passengers, and so nothing that happened in March 1910 suggested that "*a different rule was to prevail, or a different result would follow, from the identical circumstances which had previously been found to accompany nothing but safety at this point.*"[59] Only an act of God adequately explained the horrible events of that night. Should one tragedy undermine years of experience and the opinion of experts?

The court granted the rehearing *en banc*, and on May 17, 1915, both sides re-argued their cases. Following the hearing, Williams filed his final "Response to Appellant's Reply to Petition for Re-Hearing and to the Appendix to Said Reply," having not had time to respond to the appellant's reply and appendix before the rehearing.[60] In a last attempt to discount the testimony of the experienced railroad men, Williams argued that the court should consider the likelihood of slides along that section of the line rather than the testimony of the experienced men who worked for the GN. The climate and topography of the Cascades produced slides. Slides had happened before near the deadly March 1 debacle. It followed that given the force and duration of the storm, the GN should have expected a slide, in spite of the testimony of the railroad men.

Finally, on September 24, 1915, the case of *Topping v. Great Northern*

Railway Co. came to a close. The supreme court upheld its first opinion, and Topping lost his suit.[61] The expertise acquired by those who worked in the mountains about slides was reason enough to allow the highest court of the state of Washington to proclaim that only unusual natural forces had led to the deaths. The court's decision indicated that in the matter of avalanches, experience prevailed. Because they accepted that experienced men could predict slides, and because none did, the slide that had slammed the train into the ravine had to be an act of God.

The decision calls for some cynicism. The Washington supreme court had a history of conservatism and finding for big business, even after other states began to expand their liability and common carrier expectations, such as the New York case *Cormack v. New York N.H. and H.R. Co.,* cited by Williams.[62] The jury's verdict indicated that the public, at least, was questioning the lack of accountability that companies like the GN had enjoyed in the Gilded Age. As legal historian Jed Shugerman found in his study of strict liability in the Progressive Era, "The public's fears about rampant industrialization and 'non-natural' accidents" led many states' courts to begin revising their previous decisions that made proving negligence difficult.[63] Although juries did not always represent a perfect cross-section of society, and could be influenced by judge's directions, the larger historical picture supports conclusions that when the jury found for Topping it joined the shift in public sentiment that sought to expand notions of liability. As with tenants and employees, industrial relations thrust people into new relationships. In the case of passengers, technological advances that meant people traveled on mass transportation rather than under their own power pushed the boundaries of responsibility for safety beyond that of the individual. Without a doubt, these types of tragedies, of proportions and horror unheard of before the age of steamships and railways, compounded the growing concern over common carrier liability and complicated the repercussions of disasters. Also, it is intriguing to think about how in these cases local knowledge contributed to case law. In doing so, local knowledge about slides transcended the local and became part of the body of common law in America.

EIGHT

DEPARTURE FROM AVALANCHE COUNTRY

All of a sudden I heard a loud report, and instantly felt myself going swiftly
down the hill. Looking around I saw many others buried, some with their
feet out and head buried out of sight, and others vice versa. When I struck
the bottom I tried to run, but the snow caught me, and I was instantly buried
beneath 20 feet of snow and rock, being on the very verge of death by suffoca-
tion when I was reached by the rescuers.

—J. A. Raines, Chilkoot Pass, 1898

N APRIL 3, 1898, PROSPECTORS NEWLY ARRIVED ON THE WEST
side of Chilkoot Pass in Alaska—the gateway to the Klondike gold
rush—were inducted into the perils of Avalanche Country. Native
Tlingit packers warned the gold seekers away from the pass because conditions indicated a slide could happen at any time, but those anxious to get
to the goldfields did not listen. As the eager fortune hunters toiled upward,
a wall of snow swept down the pass at tremendous speed, hitting those in
its path with deadly force. The exact number killed remains uncertain, but
the estimate was somewhere near seventy dead, including twenty-three
aerial tramway construction workers.[1] Certainly these new arrivals would
have benefited from following the advice of the Tlingit people, who possessed wisdom accumulated over generations. The prospectors also could
have learned something from their counterparts in Colorado, who by the
1880s had strong convictions regarding the predictability of snowslides.

Coloradoans might have enjoyed playing in the snow, demonstrat-
ing their skills at ski races, and dancing all night at winter balls, but their
remote and lofty locales had also demanded they stay alert to the perils
of snowslides. They learned to place cabins in safe locations and moved to
protected locations when slides threatened. After slides struck, they dug out
victims, buried the dead, sought outside aid, and rebuilt their homes and
places of business. Across the Mountain West, when risks endangered a

community, members developed a range of responses that began with identifying potential problems, developing practices that tried to mitigate those problems, and coping collectively with disaster when their methods failed.[2]

The adjustments people made to live in Avalanche Country meant that participants in the industrial economy of the Mountain West remained bound to nature and possessed important knowledge about their environment. From the trappers who learned to use snowshoes to the miners and railway men who pondered the impacts of forest clear-cutting on avalanche hazard, these individuals came to know nature better. Improved knowledge led to defensive actions such as learning to ski and identifying safe zones. Over time, as more people came to work in harm's way, daring rescues and specialized knowledge about slides contributed to workplace practices that reduced danger, celebrated those who put their lives on the line, and valued those who had experience in the mountains. Families and friends who participated in rescues and public funerals reinforced the practices that supported the risky work. They also stood by that knowledge when they sought monetary compensation based on their faith that people could predict slides.

Events that began in the 1820s with the Rocky Mountain fur trade and extended into the twentieth century threw people together in Avalanche Country, a place where lack of preparedness and skills could lead to tragedy. These encounters led to exchanges of knowledge that enabled newcomers and experienced mountain people alike to better navigate their dangerous mountain home. Dependence on the help of new acquaintances sped the development of practices that allowed trappers, miners, and railroad workers to undertake greater risk with the assurance that others would help them if the need arose. This ethic reinforced a sense of responsibility that contributed to the social makeup of these communities under construction. Because winter hazards did not disappear, the risks that bound individuals together before industrial mining and railroading arrived continued to influence how mountain people understood their natural world, social spaces, and workplaces into the twentieth century.

Environmental realities invaded everyday actions in the United States and Canada. Not only in Avalanche Country, of course, but in every region that saw industrial development, men and women encountered risks and built communities that grappled with disasters and questions of responsibility and blame. Timber workers in the Northwest, coal miners in

Alberta, and dock workers in New Orleans all had to contend with place-specific challenges. And some of the worst disasters in North America occurred when humans' imperfect control of nature met urban populations—for example, the 1889 Johnstown flood in Pennsyvania caused by a broken dam that killed 2,209; the 1900 Galveston hurricane and flood in Texas that killed nearly 10,000 who did not get enough warning to evacuate before the storm; and the 1906 San Francisco earthquake and fire in California, with an estimated 3,000 dead in part due to inadequate water to quell the flames.[3] As in Avalanche Country, these tragedies raised questions about risk and responsibility in industrial society.

When employees and other victims of disasters challenged the liability laws and act-of-God rulings of the late nineteenth and early twentieth centuries they showed how legal theory had not caught up with industrial relations. Common-law doctrine, built on preindustrial work relationships, failed to address the problems of large workforces, the distance of management from work sites, and the increases in injuries and deaths caused by the failure of technology and communication.

Dissatisfaction with the system led to pressure from the bottom up in Canada and the United States. This was felt first in the local courts, but eventually in the higher courts, too.[4] In 1914, for instance, in a move away from the Revelstoke inquest's findings and the CPR's avoidance of civil cases—*Culshaw v. Crow's Nest Pass Coal Co. Ltd.*—made it to the British Columbia supreme court, where the justices upheld the lower court's decision and awarded damages to the family of a man killed by a snowslide while at work, concluding that the accident should be included under new workmen's compensation laws.[5] Then, in 1914, a national law instituted government compensation for those injured at work. In the United States, workers' compensation laws were passed state by state beginning in 1911, and would become widespread by the 1920s.

More to the point, the persistence of problems in Avalanche Country reinforces conclusions that the environment remained an integral part of the work experience there. For example, avalanches would continue to plague the southern Colorado line and contribute to the level of risk undertaken by its workers. During the winter of 1884 to 1885, the rails in this region were shut down on December 20 because of excessive snow and remained closed until July.[6] Likewise, snow blocked the line until July after the winter of 1885 to 1886, and again until April in 1887. Some years, the railroad chose to shut the line down completely, as in the winter of 1901 to 1902, deciding the expense and trouble of keeping it open were too great.[7] After a disastrous fire in 1906, a gigantic avalanche in 1909, and the collapse of part of the Alpine Tunnel in 1910, the DSP&P abandoned the route through this region. The tragedies that beset the company were not the only contributors to the DSP&P's decision to close its Alpine Tunnel spur: Competition from other railroad companies, and the fact that the cost of keeping the rails snow-free in winter exceeded the profits made along that section, also added to the company's decision.[8]

Further highlighting the persistence of winter problems were the actions by Canadian Pacific Railway (CPR) and Great Northern (GN) following the disastrous slides of 1910. In British Columbia and Washington, the companies did not close their lines like the DSP&P, but both made significant changes due to continued damage and blockades caused by slides. In 1913, three years after the Rogers Pass tragedy, the CPR began work on a tunnel that eliminated four-and-a-half miles of snowsheds and shortened the route by forty-five miles.[9] The massive construction project was concluded in August 1916, at a cost of $8.5 million to the CPR. First calling it the Rogers Pass Tunnel, then renaming it the Selkirk Tunnel, the CPR finally settled on calling it the Connaught Tunnel.[10] Such an investment by the company spoke to the importance of reducing problems with avalanches, and these adjustments indicated that snow and slides still threatened every worker and passenger on the line.

Likewise, in Washington, when the GN finished the Cascade Tunnel in 1900, it expected that many of the problems of keeping the line open in winter had ended. Yet the winter of 1910 proved this assumption wrong. As the horror of the Wellington slide showed, winter hazards still posed a threat. After the avalanche, the GN changed the name of Wellington to Tye, in an attempt to eradicate the bad associations with the name of the place. The GN took other steps to preserve its reputation as well. President James J. Hill authorized the construction of twenty-six snowsheds at a cost of more than $1.5 million. Where the slide had occurred in 1910, the GN built a 3,900-foot, double-track, concrete snowshed (which is still there today). In later years the GN built a tunnel through Windy Point, the trouble spot at Shed 3.3 where slides persisted, and protected 60 percent of the track between "Tye" and Scenic with snowsheds. Still, Stevens Pass caused problems for the line, and the company decided to do away with that route permanently. In 1929, the GN completed its rerouting, which included an eight-mile-long tunnel through the mountains and forty miles of new track.[11] As in British Columbia, such a massive undertaking obscured what should be highlighted: that industrialization did little in these places to alienate workers from their environment. In fact, for many, industrial work led to more intimate connections with the environment. The tunnels stood as more than feats of engineering: They represented stories of people struggling to apply multiple strategies to environmental problems.[12] It is equally hard to overlook the hypocrisy of the GN's actions, because the company would not have invested so much money in tunnels and snowsheds if it did not believe slides tended to fall along predictable routes.

The striking similarities among how miners, railway workers, and their communities responded to avalanche disasters, as well as how they coped with other environmental risks, led to my argument that exchanges of local knowledge became a centerpiece of the mountain experience. As the decades passed, mountain people developed increasingly sophisticated understandings of their environment based on the range of strategies they employed to offset risk, and they shared that knowledge with one another. Over time individual and community responses to environmental challenges helped people know nature through their labor and through the larger risks they confronted by living in mountainous regions. They incorporated their environmental knowledge into workplace practices such as prediction of avalanches, disaster responses like community volunteer rescues, leisure-time activities, and attempts to assign blame that could play out in legal actions.

Disaster studies in the Mountain West make clear how the movement of snow, ice, rocks, and other debris intersected with human activities and how the physical environment can influence social interactions and community development. In a complex web of encounters, people knew nature emotionally through evaluation of risk at work; the notions of responsibility they developed as a result; and the sorrow they felt when friends, family members, and coworkers were killed. The consequences of those encounters dislodge the "myth of modernity that segregated nature from culture" and lead to more complex ways of thinking about the human–nature relationship, especially under the pressures of industrialization.[13]

For outsiders, too, the ease and speed of travel in the industrial age changed the human–nature relationship. When Sarah Covington boarded the GN train in Spokane in 1910, it is unlikely she grasped the full range of disasters possible when crossing the Cascades. Her understanding of the hazards of her journey revealed themselves over the course of the storm, when the progress of the passengers slowed and after they became trapped by slides. As her predicament worsened, surely she became more conscious of how vital the trainmen's expertise was to her safety. The passengers' dependence on the trainmen, the stranded train, the collapse of the telegraph wires, and the relentless storm all increased tension inside the passenger cars. Imagine their fear when the slide came hurtling down and pushed the train off the track and into the ravine. The personal horror gives us pause, but disasters like this offer more than just a tragic story: They offer an entry point into understanding what happens when social spaces and ecological realities collide.

Disasters like these also offer a chance to rethink the human–nature relationship in other ways.[14] The fact that disasters have largely been misunderstood and treated as disconnected from historical and social forces has contributed to their ongoing impact—the escalating death tolls, medical costs, and economic losses that affect millions of people every year.[15] And disasters in the future promise to play an increasingly destructive role in North American life and in other societies around the world because of rising populations in environmentally sensitive areas, making these misunderstandings exponentially tragic. As long as corporate power, legal tradition, and the privileging of outside expertise over local knowledge stand in the way of mitigating disaster, we will miss chances to avoid deadly encounters.[16]

In the end, the many ways that mountain people learned about their environment through the work they did and the places they lived have implications beyond the Mountain West. Industrialization in Avalanche Country did not turn all of nature into a commodity, nor did it mean absolute control of nature, or that workers lost touch with their place in nature. For many, becoming an industrial worker in such circumstances put that individual in closer contact with his or her surroundings, and learning about storms, slides, and other hazards became a critical tool of survival. Beyond the obvious influence the environment had on development in Colorado, Utah, Washington, and British Columbia, assembling the layers of nature, culture, and knowledge exchange promulgated by industrial development invites further inquiry in other locations.[17]

NOTES

INTRODUCTION

1   All quotes, Charles Fox Gardiner, *Doctor at Timberline: True Tales, Travails and Triumphs of a Pioneer Colorado Physician* (Caldwell, Idaho: Caxton Printers, 1938), 8–9.

2   Betsy R. Armstrong, *Century of Struggle against Snow: A History of Avalanche Hazard in San Juan County, Colorado* (San Juan Avalanche Project, Institute of Arctic and Alpine Research, University of Colorado, 1976, Occasional Paper 18), 1.

3   "Snow & Weather, Manual & Automated Information, An Account of Snow History at Stevens Pass," available at www.stevenspass.com/Stevens/the-mountain/z-snow-science.aspx, accessed Aug. 24, 2010.

4   Letter, John C. Frémont to Jessie B. Frémont, Jan. 2–Feb. 17,1849, Taos, New Mexico, reprinted in *The Expeditions of John C. Frémont, Volume 3: From 1848–1854*, eds. Donald Jackson and Mary Lee Spence (Urbana and Chicago: University of Illinois Press, 1984).

5   Lansford W. Hastings, *Emigrants' Guide to Oregon and California* (Cincinnati: George Conclin, 1845), 24.

6   Hastings, *Emigrants' Guide*, 25.

7   Ibid., 26.

8   Ibid., 24.

9   Gardiner, *Doctor at Timberline*, 7.

10 James P. Ronda, "Passion and Imagination in the Exploration of the American West," *A Companion to the American West*, ed. William Deverell (Malden, Mass.: Blackwell Press, 2003), 53–76, 71.

11 Leadville sits at 10,152 feet above sea level.

12 Richard White, *"It's Your Misfortune and None of My Own": A New History of the American West* (Norman: University of Oklahoma Press, 1991), 184.

13 Dan Flores, "Societies to Match the Scenery: Twentieth-Century Environmen-

tal History in the American West," *A Companion to the American West,* ed. William Deverell (Blackwell Press, 2003), 257–58.

14   Karl Marx, "Economic and Philosophical Manuscripts of 1844," *The Marx-Engels Reader,* ed. Robert C. Tucker (New York: W.W. Norton, 1972), 75–77; E. P. Thompson, "Time, Work-Discipline, and Industrial Capitalism," *Past and Present* 38 (Dec. 1967): 56–97. Contemporary historians have encouraged us to rethink working people and their relationship with nature, especially Richard White, *The Organic Machine: The Remaking of the Columbia River* (New York: Hill and Wang, 1995); Karl Jacoby, *Crimes Against Nature: Squatters, Poachers, Thieves, and the Hidden History of American Conservation* (Berkeley: University of California Press, 2001); Thomas G. Andrews, *Killing for Coal: America's Deadliest Labor War* (Cambridge: Harvard University Press, 2008).

15   Josie Moore Crum, "The San Juan Country," Sarah Platt Decker Chapter of the D.A.R., *Pioneers of the San Juan Country,* Vol. 1 (Colorado Springs: Out West Printing and Stationery, 1942); Armstrong, *Century of Struggle against Snow.*

16   Day Allen Willey, "Rocky Mountain Avalanches," *Scientific American* 92 (Feb. 25, 1905): 164.

ONE. SURVIVAL STRATEGIES

Epigraph: As quoted in Elinor Wilson, *Jim Beckwourth: Black Mountain Man, War Chief of the Crows, Trader, Trapper, Explorer, Frontiersman, Guide, Scout, Interpreter, Adventurer, and Gaudy Liar* (Norman: University of Oklahoma Press, 1972), 188. Here Beckwourth was describing a type of storm the trappers called "pouderies."

1   Warren Angus Ferris, *Life in the Rocky Mountains: A Diary of Wanderings on the Sources of the Rivers Missouri, Columbia, and Colorado from February, 1830, to November, 1835,* ed. Paul C. Phillips (Denver: Old West Publishing Company, 1940), 1.

2   Ibid., 25–26, 44.

3   Russell W. Belk and Janeen Arnold Costa, "The Mountain Man Myth: A Contemporary Consuming Fantasy," *Journal of Consumer Research* 24, no. 3 (December 1998): 218–40. Belk and Costa took this statistic from William H. Goetzmann, "The Mountain Man as Jacksonian Man," *American Quarterly* 15 (Fall 1963): 402–15.

4   Sylvia Van Kirk, *Many Tender Ties: Women in Fur-Trade Society, 1670–1870* (Norman: University of Oklahoma Press, 1983).

5   Ferris, *Life in the Rocky Mountains,* lxix.

6   Carl P. Russell, *Firearms, Traps, and Tools of the Mountain Men* (New York: Alfred A. Knopf, 1967), 11.

7   Ibid.

8   Richard W. Etulain, *Beyond the Missouri: The Story of the American West* (Albuquerque: University of New Mexico Press, 2006), 121–29.

9   William R. Swagerty, "Marriage and Settlement Patterns of Rocky Mountain Trappers and Traders," *Western Historical Quarterly* 11 (April 1980): 159–80.

10   Ferris, *Life in the Rocky Mountains,* 89.

11   Ibid., 163.

12   Stanley Vestal, *Jim Bridger: Mountain Man, A Biography* (New York: William Morrow and Company, 1946), 43.

13   Ferris, *Life in the Rocky Mountains,* 3; Osborne Russell, *Journal of a Trapper,* ed. Aubrey L. Haines (Lincoln: University of Nebraska Press, 1986), 5.

14   Russell, *Journal of a Trapper,* xxi.

15   Ibid., 5.

16   Ibid., 110.

17   Ferris, *Life in the Rocky Mountains,* 74.

18   Ibid., 75.

19   James Clyman, *Journal of a Mountain Man* (Missoula, Mont.: Mountain Press, 1928), 30.

20   Ferris, *Life in the Rocky Mountains,* 76.

21   Ibid., 77.

22   Ferris usually uses the term *snowshoe* but once refers to them as "our rackets." Ibid., 244.

23   Ibid., 202.

24   Ibid., 124.

25   Ibid., 23.

26   George A. F. Ruxton, *Adventures in Mexico and the Rocky Mountains* (Glorieta, N. Mex.: Rio Grande Press, 1973), 242. As quoted in Harvey L. Carter and Marcia C. Spencer, "Stereotypes of the Mountain Man," *Western Historical Quarterly* 6 (January 1975): 17–32.

27   Washington Irving, *The Adventures of Captain Bonneville,* ed. Robert A. Rees and Alan Sandy (Philadelphia: Carey, Lea, & Blanchard, 1837; Boston: Twayne Publishers, 1977), 11.

28   Ibid., 11.

29   Russell, *Journal of a Trapper,* 95.

30   Ibid.

31   Kerry R. Oman, "Winter in the Rockies: Winter Quarters of the Mountain Men," *Montana: The Magazine of Western History* 52, no. 1 (Spring 2002): 34–47.

32   Russell, *Journal of a Trapper,* 98.

33   Ibid., 96; Oman, "Winter in the Rockies."

34   Ferris, *Life in the Rocky Mountains,* 51.

35   Ibid., 59.

36   Ibid., 5.

37   Ibid., 188.

38   Ibid.

39   Ibid., 315–16.

40   Ibid., 317.

41   Elinor Wilson, *Jim Beckwourth: Black Mountain Man, War Chief of the Crows, Trader, Trapper, Explorer, Frontiersman, Guide, Scout, Interpreter, Adventurer, and Gaudy Liar* (Norman: University of Oklahoma Press, 1972), 70–71.

42   Ray A. Billington, *America's Frontier Culture: Three Essays* (College Station: Texas A&M University Press, 1977); Swagerty, "Marriage and Settlement Patterns": 159–180; William H. Goetzmann and Harvey L. Carter, "Mountain Man Stereotypes," *Western Historical Quarterly* 6 (July 1975): 295–302; Belk and Costa, "The Mountain Man Myth": 218–40.

43   Richard M. Clokey, *William H. Ashley: Enterprise and Politics in the Trans-Mississippi West* (Norman: University of Oklahoma Press, 1980), 196–97.

44   Quoted in Swagerty, "Marriage and Settlement Patterns of Rocky Mountain Trappers and Traders," 174, from George P. Hammond, *The Adventures of Alexander Barclay, Mountain Man* (Denver: Old West Publishing Company, 1976), 42.

45   Etulain, *Beyond the Missouri*, 4–5.

46   Ibid., 127.

47   Russell, *Firearms, Traps, and Tools of the Mountain Men*, 22.

48   Bernard DeVoto, *The Year of Decision: 1846* (New York: H. Wolff, 1942).

49   Richard White, *"It's Your Misfortune and None of My Own:" A New History of the American West* (Norman: University of Oklahoma Press, 1991), 191.

50   John D. Unruh, Jr., *The Plains Across: The Overland Emigrants and the Trans-Mississippi West, 1840–60* (Urbana: University of Illinois Press, 1979), 119.

51   Ibid., 408–13.

52   Ibid., 118–20.

53   Ibid., 74.

54   Lansford W. Hastings, *Emigrants' Guide to Oregon and California* (Cincinnati: George Conclin, 1985); Edwin Bryant, *What I Saw in California*, 4th ed. (New York: D. Appleton, 1849); William Clayton, *The Latter-Day Saints' Emigrants' Guide* (St. Louis: Missouri Republican Steam Power Press—Chambers & Knapp, 1848), as cited in Unruh, *The Plains Across*, 317.

55   Ray Allen Billington, "Books that Won the West: The Guidebooks of the Forty-Niners and Fifty-Niners," *The American West* 4, no. 3 (Aug. 1967): 25–32, 72–75.

56   James Clyman, *Journal of a Mountain Man*.

57   George R. Stewart, *Ordeal by Hunger: The Story of the Donner Party* (Lincoln: University of Nebraska Press, 1986), 31.

58   Kenneth N. Owens, "The Mormon–Carson Emigrant Trail in Western History," *Montana: The Magazine of Western History* 42, no. 1 (Winter 1992), 199–211.

59   There exists some controversy over the number of people in the Donner party and about how many survived. Richard White, in *"It's Your Misfortune and None of My Own"* (207), found that of the original 89 members, 42 died and 47 lived. J. Quinn Thornton, *Oregon and California in 1848*, in *Unfortunate Emigrants: Narratives of the Donner Party*, ed. Kristin Johnson (Logan: Utah State University Press, 1996), stated that out of 80 members, 36 died and 44 lived. I have chosen to use the most recent numbers of Donald Grayson, "The Donner Party: Sex and Death on the Western Immigrant Trail," *Inside Chico State* 31, no. 15 (April 26, 2001), www.csuchico.edu/pub/inside/archive/01_04_26/02 .donnerparty.html. Grayson says the group started with 87 members, 5 died on the trail, and 35 died in the mountains, leaving 47 survivors. See also Stewart, *Ordeal by Hunger.*

60   Unruh, *The Plains Across,* 345.

61   Ibid.

62   Leonard J. Arrington and Davis Bitton, *The Mormon Experience: A History of the Latter-day Saints* (Urbana: University of Illinois Press, 1992), 134.

63   Author David Roberts puts the blame for this tragedy on Brigham Young's ambitions; see David Roberts, *Devil's Gate: Brigham Young and the Great Mormon Handcart Tragedy* (New York: Simon & Schuster, 2008).

TWO. MINERS, MAILMEN, AND PREACHERS

Epigraphs: H. G. Squier, "The Snow-Shoers of Plumas," *California Illustrated Magazine, 1891* (Feb. 1894): 318–24; *The San Juan* (Silverton, Colo., 1887).

1   Richard White, *"It's Your Misfortune and None of My Own": A New History of the American West* (Norman: University of Oklahoma Press, 1991), 191.

2   Colorado attained statehood in 1876.

3   For more, see Carl Abbott, Stephen J. Leonard, and David McComb, *Colorado: A History of the Centennial State* (Niwot: University of Colorado Press, 1994).

4   "In the San Juan," *Harper's Weekly* 27 (June 9, 1883): 365.

5   In this I mean the original boom. Alta was reborn as a ski town in the late 1930s and 1940s.

6   Anthony Will Bowman, "From Silver to Skis: A History of Alta, Utah, and Little Cottonwood Canyon, 1847–1966" (master's thesis, Utah State University, 1967), 3–4.

7   At the beginning of the Civil War, the U.S. Army had sent regular troops to Utah to monitor activities and quell any Confederate sympathies that might develop among the Mormons. In 1862, the Army replaced the troops with 750 Third California Volunteers. The volunteers prospected during their time off. By 1863, some of the volunteers had organized the Wasatch mining district, which included Little Cottonwood Canyon; Bowman, "From Silver to Skis," 12–13. See also Leonard Arrington, "Abundance from the Earth: The Beginnings of Commercial Mining in Utah," *Utah Historical Quarterly* 31 (Summer 1963): 194.

8   "Little Cottonwood Items," *Salt Lake Daily Tribune*, Jan. 23, 1874.

9   Charles Fox Gardiner, *Doctor at Timberline* (Caldwell, Idaho: Caxton Printers, 1938, 1939, 1940), 28.

10   Ibid.

11   For a series of letters on the common practice of nose-blackening in Colorado, see "Nose-Blackening as Preventive of Snow-Blindness," *Nature* 38 (May 3, 1888): 7; *Nature* 38 (May 31, 1888): 101–102; *Nature* 38 (June 21, 1888): 172; and *Nature* 40 (Sept. 5, 1889): 438.

12   John L. Dyer, *The Snowshoe Itinerant: An Autobiography* (Cincinnati: Cranston and Stowe, 1890), 216.

13   "In the San Juan."

14   Dyer, *The Snowshoe Itinerant*, 150.

15   "In the San Juan," 366.

16   Ibid.

17   J. M. Goodwin, "The Prospector," *Overland Monthly* 34 (August 1899), 165.

18   "In the San Juan," 365. See also Abbott Fay, *A History of Skiing in Colorado* (Ouray, Colo.: Western Reflections, 1999); and Annie G. Coleman, *Ski Style: Sport and Culture in the Rockies* (Lawrence: University of Kansas Press, 2004).

19   James K. Hastings, "A Winter in the High Mountains, 1871–72," *Colorado Magazine* (July 1950): 225–34. For an overview of the history of skiing in Colorado during this period, see Abbott Fay, *Ski Tracks in the Rockies: A Century of Colorado Skiing* (Louisville, Colo.: Cordillera Press, 1984), 1–8; and Jack A. Benson, "Before Skiing Was Fun," *Western Historical Quarterly* 8 (Oct. 1997): 431–42.

20   Dan De Quille (William Wright), "John A. 'Snowshoe' Thompson," *Overland Monthly* (Oct. 1886), reprinted in *Nevada Historical Review*, Vol. 2, Issue 2, 1974: 44–73

21   Gardiner, *Doctor at Timberline*, 18.

22   "In the San Juan," 365.

23   J. J. Gibbons, *In the San Juan, Colorado: Sketches* (J. J. Gibbons, 1898), 350. Dr. Gardiner also remarked on the importance of skiing.

24   A. W. Dimock, "Adventures on Skees and Snowshoes," *Country Life in America* (Dec. mid-month 1910): 185–88.

25   Ibid.

26   Needleton sits on the San Juan/La Plata County line, about ten miles south of Silverton.

27   Dimock, "Adventures on Skees and Snowshoes," 186.

28   Ibid., 185–88.

29   E. John B. Allen, "Skiing Mailmen of Mountain America: U.S. Winter Postal Service in the Nineteenth Century," *Journal of the West* 29 (1990): 76–86.

30   De Quille, "John A. 'Snowshoe' Thompson," 53.

31   Ibid.

32   Ibid., 57.

33   Allen, "Skiing Mailmen of Mountain America," 78–81.

34   James K. Hastings, "A Winter in the High Mountains, 1871–72," *Colorado Magazine* (July 1950): 232.

35   Gibbons, *In the San Juan*, 165.

36   Lulita Crawford Pritchett, ed., *Diary of Lulie Margie Crawford: A Little Girl's View of Life in the Old West, 1880–1881* (Denver: Egan Printing, 1985), 18.

37   Reprinted in ibid., 18. From the *Daily Sentinel* (Grand Junction, Colorado, 1941).

38   Pritchett, ed., *Diary of Lulie Margie Crawford*, 22–23.

39   Ibid., 23.

40   Squier, "The Snow-Shoers of Plumas": 320.

41   Ibid.

42   Ibid., 321.

43   Ibid., 319.

44   Gibbons describes a Christmas Eve mass attended by both Protestants and Catholics. *In the San Juan*, 23.

45   Dyer often felt that his lack of education was a detriment in his profession as a minister. He also felt that after spending seven years in the lead mines of Wisconsin he had a fairly realistic view of mining. He wrote that when he heard news of a big strike, his experience "prepared me to be cautious in swallowing such news" (350). Dyer, *The Snow-Shoe Itinerant*.

46   Dyer, *The Snow-Shoe Itinerant*, 124.

47   Bowman, "From Silver to Skis," 66–67.

48   Dyer, *The Snow-Shoe Itinerant*, 164.

49   Ibid., 145.

50   Malcolm J. Rohrbough, "Mining and the Nineteenth Century American West," *A Companion to the American West*, ed. William Deverell (Malden, Mass.: Blackwell, 2004), 116.

51   H. J. Hawley, "H. J. Hawley's Diary, Russell Gulch in 1860," ed. Lynn I. Perrigo, *Colorado Magazine* 31 (Oct. 1954): 140.

52   Ibid., 137.

53   Gibbons, *In the San Juan*, 121.

54   Harriet L. Wason, "The Slide at the Empire Mine," *Letters from Colorado* (Boston: Cupples and Hurd, 1887), 154–56, reprinted in *Poems of the Old West: A Rocky Mountain Anthology*, ed. Levette J. Davidson (Whitefish, Mont.: Kessinger, 2004), 37–39.

55   Robert L. Brown, *An Empire of Silver: A History of the San Juan Silver Rush* (Caldwell, Idaho: Caxton, 1965), 75.

56   Squier, "The Snow-Shoers of Plumas," 321.

57   Ibid., 322.

58   Ibid.

59   Gibbons, *In the San Juan*, 8.

60   Ibid., 33.

61   Ibid., 42.

62   Ibid., 33.

THREE. INDUSTRIAL MINING AND RISK

Epigraph: *Silverton Standard* (Colorado), April 14, 1906.

1   Mark Wyman, "Industrial Revolution in the West: Hard-Rock Miners and the New Technology," *Western Historical Quarterly* 5, no. 1 (Jan. 1974): 39-57.

2   United States Census, 1880 and 1890.

3   J. J. Gibbons, *In the San Juan, Colorado: Sketches* (J. J. Gibbons, 1898), 51.

4   Statistics compiled by Betsy Armstrong from regional newspapers. Betsy Armstrong, *Century of Struggle against Snow: A History of Avalanche Hazard in San Juan County, Colorado* (Boulder, Colo.: Institute of Arctic and Alpine Research, occasional paper, 1976), 76-77.

5   Statistics compiled by Charles L. Keller from newspaper articles. Charles L. Keller, *The Lady in the Ore Bucket: A History of Settlement and Industry in the Tri-Canyon Area of the Wasatch Mountains* (Salt Lake City: University of Utah Press, 2001), 179-82.

6   Phyllis Flanders Dorset, *The Story of Colorado's Gold and Silver Rushes* (New York: Barnes and Noble, 1994), 225.

7   Hubert Howe Bancroft, *History of Utah, 1540-1886* (San Francisco: History Company, 1889), 747.

8   Robert A. Trennert, *Riding the High Wire: Aerial Tramways in the West* (Boulder: University of Colorado Press, 2001), 58.

9   Ibid., 9.

10   Armstrong, *Century of Struggle against Snow*, 19-23.

11   Ibid., 23.

12   As quoted from *Silverton Democrat (Colorado)*, Jan. 29, 1887, in ibid., 25.

13   E. W., "From Little Cottonwood," *Salt Lake Daily Tribune and Utah Mining Gazette*, May 23, 1871.

14   *Deseret Evening News* (Salt Lake City), 1885.

15   J. M. Goodwin, "Snowslides in the Rockies; A Perilous Study," *Overland Monthly* 29 (April 1897): 384. It seems likely that Goodwin exaggerates the number of the dead.

16   James K. Hastings, "A Winter in the High Mountains, 1871-72," *Colorado Magazine* (July 1950): 225-34.

17   Special Correspondent S., "News from Little Cottonwood Canyon," *Salt Lake Daily Tribune and Utah Mining Gazette*, May 16, 1871.

18   Anthony Will Bowman, "From Silver to Skis: A History of Alta, Utah, and Little Cottonwood Canyon, 1847-1966" (master's thesis, Utah State University, 1967), 63.

19   Mark Wyman, *Hard Rock Epic: Western Miners and the Industrial Revolution, 1860-1910* (Berkeley: University of California Press, 1979), 12.

20   Gibbons, *In the San Juan*, 121.

21   "The Alta Catastrophe," *Deseret Evening News*, March 10, 1884.

22   Gibbons, *In the San Juan*, 189.

23   Elizabeth Jameson, *All That Glitters: Class, Conflict, and Community in Cripple Creek* (Urbana: University of Illinois Press, 1998), 34.

24   Ibid., 35.

25   Ibid., 36. See also Karen Buckley, *Danger, Death, and Disaster in the Crowsnest Pass Mines, 1902-1928* (Calgary: University of Calgary Press, 2004).

26   All quotes this paragraph: *San Juan Herald* (Silverton, Colorado), Jan. 27, 1887.

27   All quotes this paragraph: *Silverton Standard*, April 7, 1906.

28   *Silverton Standard*, April 14, 1906.

29   H. G. Squier, "The Snow-Shoers of Plumas," *Californian Illustrated Magazine, 1891* (Feb. 1894): 323.

30   Ibid., 323.

31   Jameson, *All That Glitters*, 36.

32   Ruth Winder Robertson, *This Is Alta* (Alta, UT: Ruth W. Robertson, 1972), 70.

33   Ibid., 69.

34   "Floating Fragments," *Deseret Evening News*, Dec. 11, 1883. Terrible slides also visited Alta in 1881. *Salt Lake Tribune*, Jan. 13-15, 1881.

35   "Editorial Notes," *Deseret Evening News*, Dec. 18, 1883.

36   *Deseret Evening News*, March 4, 1884, and March 7, 1884.

37   "An Arctic Winter," *Deseret Evening News*, March 5, 1884.

38   "Avalanche at Alta," *Deseret Evening News,* March 10, 1884.

39   "The Alta Victims," *Deseret Evening News,* March 12, 1884.

40   "The Alta Victims," *Deseret Evening News,* March 14, 1884.

41   "The Dreadful Destruction," *Ogden (Utah) Standard Examiner,* Feb. 16, 1885.

42   Ibid.

43   Robertson, *This Is Alta,* 71-74.

44   Keller, *The Lady in the Ore Bucket,* 174-75.

45   Ibid., 175.

46   Russell R. Dynes and Kathleen J. Tierney, eds., *Disasters, Collective Behavior, and Social Organization* (Newark: University of Delaware Press, 1994), 130.

47   *Silverton Standard* (Colorado), March 21, 1891.

48   Miners used the terms "great powder" or "giant powder" interchangeably with "dynamite."

49   Gibbons, *In the San Juan,* 134.

50   Day Allen Willey, "Rocky Mountain Avalanches," *Scientific American* (Feb. 25, 1905): 166.

51   Avalanche victims usually suffocate within minutes of burial. According to Ken White of the Friends of the Avalanche Center in Washington state, after fifteen minutes rescuers assume they are looking to recover bodies, not breathing victims. Ken White, interview with author, Jan. 24, 2007.

52   John W. Jenkins, *Colorado Avalanche Disasters: An Untold Story of the Old West* (Ouray, Colo.: Western Reflections, 2001), 56-70.

53   Gunther Peck, "Manly Gambles: The Politics of Risk on the Comstock Lode, 1860-1880," *Journal of Social History* 26 (Summer 1993): 701-23.

54   Dan De Quille (William Wright), "John A. 'Snowshoe' Thompson," *Overland Monthly* (Oct. 1886), as reprinted in *Nevada Historical Review* (1976), 68.

55   Squier, "The Snow-Shoers of Plumas," 318-24.

56   Ibid., 324.

57   Ibid.

58   Betsy R. Armstrong and Knox Williams, *The Avalanche Book* (Golden, Colo.: Fulcrum, 1992), 43.

59   E. R. Warren, "Snow-Shoeing in the Rocky Mountains," *Outing Magazine* 9 (Jan. 1887): 352.

60   George Root, George A. Root Collection, Stephen H. Hart Library, Colorado Historical Society, Denver, confirms that the first series of ski races held in Crested Butte were on Washington's Birthday, the winter of 1885–86.

61   Ibid.

62   Warren, "Snow-shoeing in the Rocky Mountains," 353.

63   "Little Cottonwood Items," *Salt Lake Daily Tribune,* Feb. 4, 1874.

64   "A Snow Shoe Race," *Salt Lake Daily Tribune,* Feb. 11, 1874.

65   "Alta Items," *Salt Lake Daily Tribune*, Jan. 27, 1874.

66   Hal K. Rothman, *Devil's Bargains: Tourism in the Twentieth-Century American West* (Lawrence: University Press of Kansas, 2000), 173-74.

67   A. W. Brian Simpson, *Cannibalism and the Common Law: The Story of the Tragic Last Voyage of the* Mignonette *and the Strange Legal Proceedings to Which It Gave Rise* (Chicago: University of Chicago Press, 1984).

FOUR. RAILWAY WORKERS AND MOUNTAIN TOWNS

Epigraphs: *Revelstoke Mail Herald,* March 5, 1910; and *Topping v. The GN Railway Company.* Case tried in the Superior Court of Washington in and for King County, Records of State Supreme Court Case, #11949, Washington State Archives, Olympia, Washington, 325, 326.

1   Merridan Howard, "How Railroad Men Fight Snow," *Pearson's Magazine* 5 (Jan.–June 1898): 26–34.

2   F. Lynde, "How the Railroads Fight Snow," *Munsey's Magazine* 22 (Oct. 1899–March 1900): 482.

3   Ibid., 478–86.

4   T. J. Jackson Lears, *No Place of Grace: Antimodernism and the Transformation of American Culture, 1880–1920* (Chicago: University of Chicago Press, 1981), 69.

5   As quoted in Ronald Takaki, *Strangers from a Different Shore: A History of Asian Americans* (Boston: Little, Brown, 1989), illustration, between 304 and 305.

6   "Little Cottonwood Items," *Salt Lake Daily Tribune,* Jan. 23, 1874.

7   "Little Cottonwood Items," *Salt Lake Daily Tribune,* Jan. 7, 1874.

8   Day Allen Willey, "Rocky Mountain Avalanches," *Scientific American* 92 (Feb. 26, 1905): 166.

9   "Snow Sheds: How the CPRR Crossed the Summit," http://railroad.lindahall. org/essays/innovations.html, accessed Jan. 27, 2013.

10   Anthony Will Bowman, "From Silver to Skis: A History of Alta, Utah, and Little Cottonwood Canyon, 1847–1966" (master's thesis, Utah State University, 1967), 23; *Deseret News* (Salt Lake City, Utah), Nov. 13, 1872.

11   Robert L. Brown, *Ghost Towns of the Colorado Rockies* (Caldwell, Idaho: Caxton Printers, 1968), 39–42.

12   George Root, George A. Root Collection, Stephen H. Hart Library, Colorado Historical Society, Denver.

13   As quoted in John Whelan, "Frozen Hell on Earth," *Mountain Heritage Magazine: The Journal of Rocky Mountain Life and History* 3 (Winter 2000/2001): 12–16.

14 J. Arthur Lower, *Western Canada: An Outline History* (Vancouver: Douglas and McIntyre, 1983), 120–30; Ruby Nobbs, *Rail Tales from the Revelstoke Division* (Altona, Manitoba: Friesens, 2000), 8–9.

15 Whelan, "Frozen Hell on Earth," 13; John G. Woods, *Snow War: An Illustrated History of Rogers Pass, Glacier National Park, B.C.*, ed. John S. Marsh, (N.P.P.A.C. [Parks Canada], 1983), 5.

16 Lynde, "How the Railroads Fight Snow," 483.

17 Ibid., 479.

18 Greville Palmer, "'Snow Bucking' in the Rocky Mountains," *Longman's Magazine* 5 (Feb. 1885): 422–31, 431. See also Howard, "How Railway Men Fight Snow," 26–34, for descriptions of snowsheds, snow fences, and plows.

19 Fred Beckey, *Range of Glaciers: The Exploration and Survey of the Northern Cascade Range* (Portland: Oregon Historical Society, 2003), 221.

20 Ibid., 257–68.

21 Lynde, "How the Railroads Fight Snow," 480.

22 Palmer, "'Snow Bucking' in the Rocky Mountains," 422–31.

23 Lynde, "How the Railroads Fight Snow," 481.

24 Cy Warman, "The Battle of the Snow-Plows: A True Story of Railroading in the Rocky Mountains," *McClure's Magazine* 8 (Nov. 1896): 92–96.

25 Lynde, "How the Railroads Fight Snow," 481.

26 Ibid., 479–83.

27 Ibid., 481.

28 See Statistics Canada, www.statcan.gc.ca/pub/11-516-x/sectiona/A2_14-eng.csv, accessed March 28, 2010.

29 Howard, "How the Railroad Men Fight Snow," 26.

30 J. J. Gibbons, *In the San Juan, Colorado: Sketches* (J. J. Gibbons, 1898), 120.

31 Lawrence M. Friedman and Jack Ladinsky, "Social Change and the Law of Industrial Accidents," *Columbia Law Review* 67 (Jan. 1967): 50–82, 60.

32 "The Almighty's Will," *Mail-Herald* (Revelstoke, B.C.), March 9, 1910; Howard Zinn, *A People's History of the United States* (New York: Harper Perennial, 1980), 272.

33 John Williams-Searle, "Courting Risk: Disability, Masculinity, and Liability on Iowa's Railroads, 1868–1900," *Annals of Iowa* 58 (Winter 1999): 24–77.

34 Shelton Stromquist, *A Generation of Boomers: The Pattern of Railroad Labor Conflict in Nineteenth-Century America* (Urbana: University of Illinois Press, 1987), 142–46.

35 Nobbs, *Rail Tales from the Revelstoke Division.*

36 Ibid., 25.

37 "A Terrible Accident," *Revelstoke Herald*, Feb. 1, 1899.

38 "Rogers' Pass Tragedy," *Revelstoke Herald*, Feb. 4, 1899.

39 Nobbs, *Rail Tales from the Revelstoke Division*, 25-26.

40 "Rogers' Pass Tragedy."

41 "An Awful Avalanche," *Kootenay Mail*, Feb. 4, 1899.

42 Ibid.

43 Ibid.

44 Jeremy Mouat, *Roaring Days: Rossland's Mines and the History of British Columbia* (Vancouver: University of British Columbia Press, 1995), 111-14, discusses how the language that applauded masculine skills in periodicals and literature was repeated and reinforced by miners in Rossland, B.C., much like the railroad workers in Revelstoke did.

45 Carlos A. Schwantes, *Radical Heritage: Labor, Socialism, and Reform in Washington and British Columbia, 1885-1917* (Moscow: University of Idaho Press, 1994).

46 Edmund E. Pugsley, "Some Had Luck," *Railroad Magazine* 48 (Feb. 1949): 70-78.

47 *Mail-Herald*, Feb. 26, 1910.

48 Ibid.

49 Pugsley, "Some Had Luck," 70-78.

50 John Anderson, as told to Elvina L. Duncan, "Death Rode the Snows," *True West* 12 (Sept.-Oct. 1965): 44-45, 62-63.

51 Cecil Clark, "Disaster at Avalanche Mountain," *Daily Colonist (Victoria, B.C.)*, Nov. 15, 1959.

52 "Idaho Town Swept off Map," *Mail-Herald*, March 2, 1910.

53 "Awful Disaster," *Mail-Herald*, March 5, 1910; Pugsley, "Some Had Luck," 74.

54 D. G. Scott Calder, "The Reminiscences of Major D. G. Scott Calder, E.D.," History: Railroad File, Canadian Parks Archives, Revelstoke, B.C.

55 "Story of the Passengers," reprinted in *Rogers Pass Herald,* May 28, 1981.

56 Donald G. Scott Calder, "The Rogers Pass Snowslide," Sept. 1974, Railway Slides File, Revelstoke Museum and Archives, Revelstoke, B.C. (hereafter cited as RMA).

57 Reports vary on the number of men killed in the slide. In 1998, archivist Cathy English of the Revelstoke Museum culled various sources with numbers ranging from 58 to 66 men to determine the actual number killed in the slide. After reviewing newspaper articles, CPR correspondences, and funeral invoices, she determined that 58 deaths is the most accurate count. From "Research Report Regarding the Snowslide at Rogers Pass, March 4th, 1910." Railway Slides file, RMA.

58 "The Luck of LaChance," CBC interview, 1979, Railroad History File, Parks Canada, Revelstoke, B.C.

59 Ibid.

60 "Hundreds of Workmen Dig for Buried Comrades," *Vancouver Daily Province*, March 5, 1910. "Awful Avalanche of Death," *Mail-Herald*, March 5, 1910, reported that at least 500 men arrived.

61 "The Luck of LaChance"; "Awful Avalanche of Death."

62 "Volunteers" did get some compensation from the CPR, along with letters of thanks. Calder, "Reminiscences."

63 Calder remembers, too, that "as a result of the Slide the CPR wisely built the Roger's Pass tunnel." Calder, "Reminiscences."

64 "Coroner's Inquest," *Mail-Herald*, March 12, 1910.

65 Ibid.

66 Ibid.

67 Ibid.

68 Ibid.

69 Ibid.

70 Ibid.

71 Ibid.

72 Ibid.

73 Form 395, March 7, 1910, CPR, Revelstoke Divisional Records, 1909–1975, RMA.

74 This name is sometimes spelled "Moffat" in letters and other records.

75 Letter, Anne Moffatt to Tom Kilpatrick, May 2, 1910, CPR, Revelstoke Divisional Records, 1909–1975, RMA.

76 In general, British Columbia was a xenophobic place. See Jeremy Mouat, *Roaring Days*; Schwantes, *Radical Heritage*; and Takaki, *Strangers from a Different Shore*. At this time, Asian Indians immigrated to the United States, Canada, British West Indies, Uganda, Maritius, and British Guiana. They found themselves especially marginalized in British Columbia, where white workers worried that the immigrants would drive down wages. Immigration came almost to a halt in 1914, when more restrictive immigration laws went into effect.

77 "Last Tribute to Rogers Pass Victims," *Mail-Herald,* March 23, 1910.

78 Letter, Mehar Singh to Superintendent Kilpatrick, undated, Railway Slides File, RMA.

79 Ibid.

80 All quotes this paragraph, ibid.

81 "Awful Avalanche of Death."

82 Ibid.

83 "Hundreds of Workmen Dig for Buried Comrades," *Vancouver Daily Province*, March 5, 1910.

84 *Mail-Herald,* March 12, 1910.

85 "Awful Avalanche of Death."

86 *Calgary Daily Herald,* March 7, 1910.

87   Ibid.

88   Ibid.

89   Ibid.

90   Ibid.

91   Ibid.

92   "The Almighty's Will."

93   Letter, Moffatt to Kilpatrick, May 2, 1910.

94   Letter, Tom Kilpatrick to Anne Moffatt, March 16, 1910. CPR, Revelstoke Divisional Records, 1909–1975, RMA.

95   "The Almighty's Will."

96   "Public Funeral," *Mail-Herald*, March 19, 1910.

97   "Last Tribute to Rogers Pass Victims," *Mail-Herald*, March 23, 1910.

98   Memorial Service Pamphlet, Railway Slides File, RMA.

99   "Last Tribute to Rogers Pass Victims."

100 Ibid.

101 Ibid.

102 Karen Buckley, *Danger, Death and Disaster in the Crowsnest Pass Mines, 1902-1928* (Calgary: University of Calgary Press, 2004), 87–140.

FIVE. WHO'S TO BLAME?

Epigraph: 13 S. Ct. 333 (1893).

1   53 Pac. Rptr. 518, 518–20 (1893).

2   Ibid.

3   Mark Wyman, *Hard Rock Epic: Western Miners and the Industrial Revolution, 1860-1910* (Berkeley: University of California Press, 1979), 142.

4   James W. Ely, *Railroads and American Law* (Lawrence: University of Kansas Press, 2001).

5   "Out of the Drifts," *Denver Tribune*, March 13, 1884. Not completely altruistic, the citizens who went to Woodstock requested payment from Superintendent Smith of the DSP&P.

6   John W. Jenkins, *Colorado Avalanche Disasters: An Untold Story of the Old West* (Ouray, Colo.: Western Reflections, 2001), 50–51.

7   "Out of the Drifts."

8   M. C. Poor, *Denver, South Park and Pacific* (DSP&P) (Denver: Rocky Mountain Railroad Club, 1976), 349. In all thirteen people died in the slide; the last body was not found until spring.

9   The deceased Doyle children were as follows: Martin Doyle (23), Andrew Doyle (19), Katy Doyle (18), Marcella Doyle (14), Maggie Doyle (12), Christopher Doyle (10). Poor, *Denver, South Park and Pacific,* 349.

10   The article reprinted in Poor, *Denver, South Park and Pacific,* lists Celia as a
      niece, not a fiancée.

11   Poor, *Denver, South Park and Pacific,* 351.

12   Jed Handelsman Shugerman, "The Floodgates of Strict Liability: Bursting Res-
      ervoirs and the Adoption of *Fletcher v. Rylands* in the Gilded Age," *Yale Law
      Journal* 110, no. 2 (Nov. 2000): 333–77.

13   Wyman, *Hard-Rock Epic,* 142, explains that by the 1890s, a "jurors' rebellion"
      saw juries finding for employees and awarding them larger and larger compen-
      sation packages.

14   147 U.S. Reporter at 413–431 (Oct. 1892).

15   Ibid., 419.

16   This did not appear as testimony at the trial but rather as a matter of local
      knowledge. Poor, *Denver, South Park and Pacific,* 351.

17   147 U.S. Reporter at 413.

18   Morton J. Horwitz, *The Transformation of American Law, 1870–1960* (Oxford:
      Oxford University Press, 1992).

19   147 U.S. Reporter at 422.

20   135 Mass. 380, cited in 147 U.S. Reporter at 424–25.

21   134 Mass. 357, cited in 147 U.S. Reporter at 426–27.

22   2 Wheat. 178, cited in 147 U.S. Reporter at 428–29.

23   147 U.S. Reporter at 429.

24   Ibid.

25   Ibid., 430.

26   Ibid., 423.

27   See Ted Steinberg, *Acts of God: The Unnatural History of Natural Disasters in
      America* (Oxford: Oxford University Press, 2000); Kathleen J. Tierney, "Toward
      a Critical Sociology of Risk," *Sociological Forum* 14 (June 1999): 215–42.

28   135 Mass. at 380.

29   Letter, William I. Briggs to Tom Kilpatrick, April 26, 1910, CPR, Revelstoke
      Divisional Records, 1909–1975, RMA.

30   Letter, Tom Kilpatrick to W. I. Briggs, April 28, 1910, ibid.

31   Letter, W. H. D'Arcy, general claims agent, to T. Kilpatrick, superintendent,
      July 25, 1910, CPR, Revelstoke Divisional Records, 1909–1975, RMA.

32   Ibid.

33   Letter, W. H. D'Arcy, general claims agent, to Wellander's [a foreman's] widow,
      CPR, Revelstoke Divisional Records, 1909–1975, RMA; Letter, W. H. D'Arcy,
      general claims agent, to Johnson's [a foreman] family, CPR, Revelstoke Divi-
      sional Records, 1909–1975, RMA; W. H. D'Arcy, general claims agent, to Mrs.
      McLennan, CPR, Revelstoke Divisional Records, 1909–1975, RMA.

34 Letter, Kilpatrick to Busteed, Dec. 9, 1910, CPR, Revelstoke Divisional Records File, 1909–1975, RMA.

35 Letter, Tom Kilpatrick to Anne Moffatt, March 16, 1910, CPR, Revelstoke Divisional Records File, 1909–1975, RMA; Letter, Tom Kilpatrick to Norman Wilson, Esq., March 26, 1910, CPR, Revelstoke Divisional Records File, 1909–1975, RMA; Letter, Tom Kilpatrick to Norman Wilson, Esq., May 10, 1910, CPR, Revelstoke Divisional Records File, 1909–1975, RMA; Letter, Tom Kilpatrick to F. Baker, Esq., May 26, 1910, CPR, Revelstoke Divisional Records File, 1909–1975, RMA.

36 Telegram, John Anderson to Tom Kilpatrick, March 13, 1910; Letter, Tom Kilpatrick to J. A. Renaud, April 21, 1910, CPR, Revelstoke Divisional Records, 1909–1975, RMA.

37 All quotes this paragraph from letter, Tom Kilpatrick to F. F. Busteed, Esq., May 7, 1910, Railway Slides File, RMA.

38 CPR, Revelstoke Divisional Records, 1909–1975, RMA.

39 Verdict of the Second Inquest, signed by members of the jury, Railway Slides File, RMA.

SIX. DISASTER IN THE CASCADES

Epigraph: *William Topping by W. V. D. Topping, guardian ad litem, v. Great Northern Railway Company, a corporation,* Case No. 94511, Superior Court of the State of Washington, Spokane County (moved to King County), King County Court House, Clerk's Records, Seattle, Washington.

1 S. J. Covington Diary, Washington Misc., Ms. Collection (T-166), Box 2 Folder 21, Washington State Historical Society, Tacoma, Washington.

2 Ibid.

3 Gary Krist, *The White Cascade: The Great Northern Railway Disaster and America's Deadliest Avalanche* (New York: Henry Holt, 2007), 149.

4 Ibid., 253–58.

5 Testimony taken before Coroner J.C. Snyder, from transcript of Wellington Slide inquest, March 13, 1910, 153. Transcript of Wellington Slide inquest, Robert Kelly, private collection, Renton, Washington (hereinafter *Inquest*).

6 Ibid., 266.

7 Ibid., 213–219.

8 Ibid., 436.

9 Krist, *The White Cascade,* 253–58.

10 F. Lynde, "How the Railroads Fight Snow," *Munsey's Magazine* 22 (Oct. 1899 to March 1900): 478–86.

11 Wellington, *Inquest,* 424.

12   Ibid., 67.

13   Ibid, 418.

14   For White's full testimony, see Ibid., 418–452.

15   Ibid., 461.

16   Ibid., 254, 257.

17   Ibid., 515.

18   *William Topping, W. V. D. Topping guardian ad litem v. Great Northern Railway Company, a corporation,* Superior Court of the State of Washington, In and For King Country, 87 Wash. 702 (1910) (hereinafter *Topping v. Great Northern Railway*).

19   Wellington *Inquest,* 19.

20   Ibid., 21.

21   From O'Neill's testimony, Trial Transcript, *Topping v. Great Northern Railway,* 485–611.

22   Wellington, *Inquest,* 481.

23   Ibid., 485.

24   Ibid., 486.

25   Ibid., 396.

26   Wellington *Inquest,* 386.

27   Ibid., 525.

28   Transcript, *Topping v. Great Northern Railway,* 325, 326.

29   Wellington, *Inquest,* 33.

30   Ibid., 396.

31   Ibid., 385.

32   Ibid., 385.

33   Ibid., 391.

34   Ibid., 93.

35   Ibid., 93.

36   Ibid., 108.

37   Ibid., 279, 284, 308.

38   "Coroner's Inquest," *Mail-Herald* (Revelstoke, B.C.), March 12, 1910.

39   *Calgary Daily Herald,* March 8, 1910.

40   Wellington, *Inquest,* 350.

41   Ibid., 397.

42   Ibid., 525.

43   Ibid., 313–314.

44   Ibid., 314.

45   Ibid., 317.

46   Carlos A. Schwantes, *Radical Heritage: Labor, Socialism, and Reform in Wash-*

ington *and British Columbia, 1885–1917* (Moscow: University of Idaho Press, 1994).

47   Shelton Stromquist, *A Generation of Boomers: The Pattern of Railroad Labor Conflict in Nineteenth-Century America* (Urbana: University of Illinois Press, 1993), 31–35, 132, 274.

48   Wellington, *Inquest*, 530–31.

49   "Second Inquest—Rogers Pass Disaster—Verdict of Accidental Death," *Mail-Herald*, March 16,1910.

50   Wellington, *Inquest*, 530–31.

51   Ruby El Hult, *Northwest Disaster: Avalanche and Fire* (Portland, Or.: Binford and Mort, 1975), 94.

52   Krist, *The White Cascade*, 222.

53   Ibid., 223.

54   James W. Ely, *Railroads and American Law* (Lawrence: University of Kansas Press, 2001).

SEVEN. *TOPPING V. GREAT NORTHERN RAILWAY COMPANY*

Epigraph: Transcript of Testimony and Proceedings: *William Topping v. G. N. Ry. Co.*, Records of State Supreme Court, Cast # 11949, Washington State Archives, Olympia, Washington, 857 (hereinafter Transcript, *Topping v. Great Northern*).

1   *William Topping, by W. V. D. Topping, guardian ad litem, v. Great Northern Railway Company*, a corporation, Case No. 94511, Superior Court of the State of Washington, Spokane County (moved to King County), King County Court House, Clerk's Records, Seattle, Washington (hereafter *Topping v. Great Northern*), 1913.

2   Gary Krist, *The White Cascade: The Great Northern Railway Disaster and America's Deadliest Avalanche* (New York: Henry Holt, 2007), 223.

3   *Topping v. Great Northern.*

4   Morton J. Horwitz, *The Transformation of American Law, 1870–1960* (Oxford: Oxford University Press, 1992); Jed Handelsman Shugerman, "The Floodgates of Strict Liability: Bursting Reservoirs and the Adoption of *Fletcher v. Rylands* in the Gilded Age," *Yale Law Journal* 110, no. 2 (Nov. 2000): 333–77.

5   *Topping v. Great Northern.*

6   Gary Krist suggested that the witnesses had had several years to marinate on events, and the GN had had several years to align all the versions of the days before the slide by the time the case went to trial. From the author's conversation with Krist, who wrote *The White Cascade: The Great Northern Railway Disaster and America's Deadliest Avalanche.*

7   Krist, *The White Cascade*, 151.

8   The trial transcripts, which became part of the evidence for the appeal, show
     that only eleven of the plaintiff's witnesses and thirty-two of the defendant's
     actually testified. The eleven who did appear for the plaintiff included two who
     appeared at the inquest: passenger Henry White and Wellington hotel propri-
     etor Susan Bailets. Anna Gray, a passenger on the train, also testified, as did
     the coroner, Dr. J. C. Snyder. Other witnesses for the plaintiff included Kerwin
     Stuht, an insurance man who testified on life expectancy; H. L. Toles, who
     photographed the scene; longtime Washington resident James Lydon; railway
     mail clerk A. B. Hensel; and longtime Cascade Mountains resident Andrew
     Burbank. See Transcript *Topping vs. Great Northern.*

9   Trial Transcript, *Topping v. Great Northern*, 19.

10   Ibid., 192.

11   Ibid., 223.

12   Ibid., 325, 326.

13   Ibid., 355–73.

14   Ibid., 779–803.

15   J. H. O'Neill: "experienced railroad man, and familiar with winter condi-
     tions . . . that it was impossible by human means to have removed said train";
     J. J. Dowling: "experienced in similar work . . . that he believes it would have
     been impossible by any means known to railroad science to clear said track";
     J. C. Wright: "experienced railroad man"; D. Tegtmeier: "familiar with snow-
     slides"; Walter Vogle: "experienced railroad man and familiar with condi-
     tions in the Cascade Mountains"; Robert Miles: "eight years' experience in
     railroading"; J. R. Meath: that "there was more than ample coal to last through
     any blockade"; M. O. White: "that said hillside is free from the conditions
     which have heretofore made slide possible in his experience"; R. M. Loville:
     "is familiar with snow slides and the conditions causing them"; H. L. Wertz:
     passenger, that immense amount of snow smothered the rails and prevented
     movement; Joe Stafford: "six years experience"; Homer Purcell: "that a terrific
     electrical storm was raging at the time"; Percy Higga (spelling uncertain):
     "that on the night preceding the snow slide there was a heavy and continuous
     rainfall, of such violence as he had never before seen in the mountains . . . that
     he is familiar with the hillside . . . that said hillside was and still is covered with
     quite a thick stand of dead timber, and said hillside was not one which slide
     might reasonably be expected"; Robert Schwartz: "that he has been famil-
     iar with storms and winter conditions at Wellington for ten years"; George
     Loveberry: a passenger "familiar with winter storms . . . that the storm raging
     during said blockade was the longest and most severe storm ever witnessed";
     Thomas McIntyre: "seventeen years' railroad experience"; Hagan Anderson: at
     Wellington for ten years and familiar with slides, "that said slide was entirely

different from all other slides which he has seen"; Frank Ritter: passenger, that heaps of snow obstructed the rails and that no matter how fast they shoveled, the men could not keep up with the piling drifts; John A. Fick: "believed that it was started by said thunder storm"; C. E. Anderson: with eight years' experience "has seen no fire in the timber where the slide occurred"; Ross Phillips: "five years"; Floyd Stanley Funderbuck: the "supply of coal at Wellington [was] sufficient to meet any previously known emergencies"; Joe Beuezer: a section laborer for three years, "That no considerable number of laborers quit work until after said rotaries were stalled, and that at that time said laborers could have accomplished nothing toward moving the train"; J. O'Bryan: "eighteen years' railroad experience," and "familiar with snow storms"; E. Knowlee: "familiar with the hills"; Thomas O'Malley: "thirty years' railroad experience . . . familiar with winter storms," that he could not remember any slides or a fire on the hillside in the last few years; John D. Churchill: the tracks had untold amounts of snow and debris on them; Michael Ryan: "sixteen years in the Cascade Mountains . . . That there has been no fire upon the hillside . . . That the slide which occurred on March 1st broke off in a long line across the hillside, leaving a bank several feet high, and that this would not have occurred in the absence of some unusual disturbance"; John S. Rogers: passenger, that "most of said snow fell after the arrival of said train at Wellington"—along with around twenty other witnesses who supported the GN's defense. Point by point, the witnesses would swear in court that the GN had done all it could to clear the tracks, no coal shortage existed, the labor strike had not caused the blockade, no one knew of a slide ever happening in that location, no fire had cleared the slope and made it more susceptible to slides, and only a freak event, such as the thunder storm, could explain the slides occurrence. Ibid, for all quotes.

16 Ibid., 852.

17 Ibid., 853.

18 Ibid., *857.*

19 Ibid.

20 Ibid.

21 Ibid.

22 For full case reports see *Denver, South Park, and Pacific Railway Co. v. Andrews,* 53 Pac. Rep. 518–20 (Colo. Ct. Appeals, 1898); *Blythe et al. v. Denver, South Park, and Pacific Railway Co.,* 15 Colo. 339 (Colo. S. Ct. 1891); *Denver, South Park, and Pacific Railway Co. v. Pilgrim,* 47 Pac. 657–60 (Colo. Ct. Appeals, 1897).

23 F. V. Brown and F. G. Dorety, "Brief of Appellant," Case No. 11949, Supreme Court of the State of Washington, 54.

24 Ibid.

25 Ibid.

26 Ibid., 55.

27 Ibid., 59.

28 "The above rule that, where the immediate cause of the damage is the 'act of God,' the burden is upon the plaintiff to show concurring negligence, is very analogous to, if not directly deducible from, the rule established by the Supreme Court of this state regarding the doctrine of *res ipsa loquiter* and the presumption of negligence." The "proof that the accident happened will amount to a *prima facie* case of negligence *only when 'the producing cause of the injury is under the control of the defendant* and the accident is of such a nature that it would not ordinarily occur except form the lack of due care.'" Ibid., 68–69.

29 F. V. Brown and F. G. Dorety, "Brief of Appellant," 72.

30 Ibid., 103.

31 Ibid., 231.

32 Ibid., 237–57.

33 Fred M. Williams and L. F. Chester, "Brief of Respondent," Case No. 11949, Supreme Court of the State of Washington, 13.

34 Ibid., 14.

35 Ibid., 27–28.

36 Ibid., 28.

37 Ibid., 38. Emphasis in original.

38 "Hundreds of Workmen Dig for Buried Comrades," *Vancouver Daily Province*, March 5, 1910.

39 Testimony Taken before Coroner J. C. Snyder, Wellington, *Inquest*, March 13, 1910, 525.

40 Fred M. Williams and L. F. Chester, "Brief of Respondent," 110.

41 F. V. Brown and F. G. Dorety, "Reply Brief of Appellant," 15.

42 Ibid., 70.

43 Ibid., 101.

44 Washington Reports, 81, Cases Determined in the Supreme Court of Washington, Aug. 1, 1914–Sept. 26, 1914 (Seattle and San Francisco: Bancroft-Whitney, 1915), 169. See also *Lynch v. Ninemire Packing Co.*, 63 Wash. 423, 115 Pac. 838 (Wash. S. Ct., 1912).; *Lewinn v. Murphy*, 63 Wash. 356, 115 Pac. 740, Ann. Cas. 1912 D. 433 (Wash. S. Ct., 1911).

45 See *Cormack v. New York*, N.H. & H.R. Co., 24 L.R.A. (N.S.) 1209, cited in *Washington Reports*, 81, Cases Determined in the Supreme Court of Washington, 1, Aug. 1, 1914–Sept. 26, 1914, 171.

46 *Denver and R. G. R. Co. v. Andrews*, 53 Pac. 518–20.

47   As quoted in *Washington Reports*, 81, Cases Determined in the Supreme Court of Washington, Aug. 1, 1914–Sept. 26, 1914, 172.

48   See *Gillespie v. St. Louis, K.C. & N.R. Co., Jones v. Minneapolis & St. L. R. Co.,* etc., as cited in *Washington Reports*, 81, Cases Determined in the Supreme Court of Washington, Aug. 1, 1914–Sept. 26, 1914, 172.

49   Washington Reports, 81, Cases Determined in the Supreme Court of Washington, Aug. 1, 1914–Sept. 26, 1914, 173.

50   Ibid.

51   Ibid., 176.

52   Ibid., 177.

53   "Petition for Rehearing," Case No. 11949, Supreme Court of the State of Washington, Sept. 9, 1914, 1.

54   Ibid., 2-3.

55   Ibid.

56   Ibid., 46.

57   Ibid., 70.

58   Ibid., 70. *Ipse dixit* translates to "he himself said it," a term used by courts to mean the only proof of a fact that exists is that someone said it did—in other words, an arbitrary or dogmatic statement.

59   "Reply to Petition for Rehearing," Case No. 11949, Supreme Court of the State of Washington, May 17, 1915; "Appendix to Reply to Petition for Rehearing," Case No. 11949, Supreme Court of the State of Washington, May 17, 1915, 106.

60   "Response to Appellant's Reply to Petition for Re-hearing and to the Appendix to Said Reply," Case No. 11949, Supreme Court of the State of Washington, June 25, 1915.

61   The decision of the rehearing *en banc* is found in Case No. 94511, Superior Court of King County, Washington, Nov. 8, 1915.

62   *Cormack v. New York N. H. and H. R. Co.,* 196 N.Y. 442 (N.Y. 1909).

63   Shugerman, "The Floodgates of Strict Liability," 373.

EIGHT. DEPARTURE FROM AVALANCHE COUNTRY

Epigraph: "Horror of the Dyea Trail," *The New York Times*, April 10, 1898.

1   "Yukon College: Research Publications," www.taiga.net/yourYukon/col465.html, accessed April 15, 2012; Robert A. Trennert, *Riding the High Wire: Aerial Mine Tramways in the West* (Boulder: University of Colorado Press, 2001), 42.

2   Karen Buckley, *Danger, Death, and Disaster in the Crowsnest Pass Mines, 1902–1928* (Calgary: University of Calgary Press, 2004), xvii.

3   Ballard C. Campbell, ed. *Disasters, Accidents, and Crises in American History* (New York: Facts on File, 2008).

4   Nan Goodman, *Shifting the Blame: Literature, Law, and the Theory of Accidents in Nineteenth-Century America* (New York: Routledge, 1998); Jed Handelsman Shugerman, "The Floodgates of Strict Liability: Bursting Reservoirs and the Adoption of *Fletcher v. Rylands* in the Gilded Age," *Yale Law Journal* 110, no. 2 (Nov. 2000): 333–77.

5   *Culshaw v. Crow's Nest Pass Coal Co., Ltd.*, 14 D.L.R. 25.

6   George A. Root Collection, Stephen H. Hart Library, Colorado Historical Society, Denver, Colorado.

7   M. C. Poor, *The Denver, South Park, and Pacific* (Denver: Rocky Mountain Railroad Club, 1976), 348.

8   Robert L. Brown, *Ghost Towns of the Colorado Rockies* (Caldwell, Idaho: Caxton Printers, 1968) 42; Poor, *The Denver, South Park and Pacific*, 367.

9   Ruby Nobbs, *Rail Tales from the Revelstoke Division* (Altona, Manitoba: Friesens, 2000), 61.

10   Ibid., 61. Gary G. Backler, "The C.P.R.'s Capacity and Investment Strategy in Rogers Pass, B.C., 1882–1916," master's thesis, University of British Columbia, 1981, wrote about the decision made by the CPR to build the Connaught Tunnel and argued that "the principal economic benefit of the project was the savings in train-haulage costs, and not the savings in the cost of avalanche defense" (iv). See also Gary G. Backler and Trevor D. Heaver, "The Timing of a Major Investment in Railway Capacity: CPR's 1913 Connaught Tunnel Decision," *Business History* 24 (Fall 1982): 300–14. He argues against works that claim avalanches were the primary reason the CPR decided to build the tunnel: Nobbs, *Rail Tales*; P. Mason, "89 Over the Top," *Canadian Rail* 257 (June 1973): 175; John G. Woods, *Snow War: An Illustrated History of Rogers Pass, Glacier National Park* (National and Provincial Parks Association of Canada, 1983). Backler argued that the operating-cost savings were the primary reason, and the elimination of snow-related costs "incidental" (362). Backler erred in his calculations regarding the cost to the CPR when men lost their lives in slides, however. An average of seven or so employees were killed on the line each year; the average payout was only $500, or sometimes nothing at all if the person killed was an Asian laborer (approximately 236 deaths between 1883 and 1916). Although such payouts were minuscule in terms of the CPR's budget, Backler fails to account for the fact that changes in Canadian labor law put the CPR on less solid ground in terms of avoiding liability and civil suits.

11   The federal government also responded to the accident. Congress approved a doubling of the $1,000 paid to the families of mailmen killed at work. The postal employees union, the Railway Mail Association, issued $4,000 to the few mailmen who survived. Fred Beckey, *Range of Glaciers: The Exploration and*

Survey of the Northern Cascade Range (Portland: Oregon Historical Society Press, 2003), 269–70.

12   Mark Carey, *In the Shadow of Melting Glaciers: Climate Change and Andean Society* (New York: Oxford University Press, 2010), discusses how locals do not always reject outside help or privilege local knowledge exclusively over outside experts.

13   Julie Cruikshank, *Do Glaciers Listen? Local Knowledge, Colonial Encounters, and Social Imagination* (Vancouver: University of British Columbia Press, 2005), 19–20.

14   Beginning with Karl Marx, "Economic and Philosophical Manuscripts of 1844," *The Marx-Engels Reader*, ed. Robert C. Tucker (New York: W.W. Norton, 1972), 75–77, many historians have argued that the industrial process alienated workers from their environment and turned nature into a commodity. See Walter Prescott Webb, *The Great Plains* (Lincoln and London: University of Nebraska Press, 1931), 271, in which he saw changes as part of the "economic conquest" of nature that characterized the Industrial Revolution; William Cronon, *Changes in the Land: Indians, Colonists, and the Ecology of New England* (New York: Hill and Wang, 1983); Carolyn Merchant, *Ecological Revolutions: Nature, Gender, and Science in New England* (Chapel Hill: University of North Carolina Press, 1989); and Donald Worster, *Rivers of Empire: Water, Aridity, and the Growth of the American West* (New York: Oxford University Press, 1985), 5, referred to the primary relationship that guided people's use of nature as the capitalistic ecological revolution, attributable to participation in a capitalist economy, or predicated on a "managerial relationship with nature," respectively. William Cronon, in *Nature's Metropolis: Chicago and the Great West* (New York: W. W. Norton, 1991), again links economic and ecological changes, with a view to controlling and using nature as the primary cultural influence in how people understood the environment. David Igler, *Industrial Cowboys: Miller & Lux and the Transformation of the Far West, 1850–1920* (Berkeley: University of California Press, 2001); Kathleen A. Brosnan, *Uniting Mountain & Plain: Cities, Law, and Environmental Change Along the Front Range* (Albuquerque: University of New Mexico Press, 2002); and Kathryn Morse, *The Nature of Gold: An Environmental History of the Klondike Gold Rush* (Seattle: University of Washington Press, 2003), all more recent works, make similar arguments.

15   See Ted Steinberg, *Acts of God: the Unnatural History of Natural Disasters in America* (Oxford: Oxford University Press, 2000), xii; Anthony Oliver Smith, *Catastrophe and Culture: The Anthropology of Disaster* (Santa Fe, N. Mex.: School for Advanced Research Press, 2002); Kevin Rozario, *The Culture of Calamity: Disaster and the Making of Modern America* (Chicago: University of

Chicago Press, 2007); Mark Carey, *In the Shadow of Melting Glaciers: Climate Change and Andean Society* (New York: Oxford University Press, 2010); Susan L. Cutter, ed., *American Hazardscapes: The Regionalization of Hazards and Disasters* (Washington, D.C.: Joseph Henry Press, 2001); Russell R. Dynes and Kathleen J. Tierney, eds., *Disasters, Collective Behavior, and Social Organization* (Newark: University of Delaware Press, 1994), 130; Ben Wisner, Piers Blaikie, Terry Cannon, and Ian Davis, *At Risk: Natural Hazards, People's Vulnerability and Disasters,* 2nd ed. (London: Routledge, 1994).

16 See Mike Davis, *Dead Cities* (New York: New Press, 2002), 8; John Bellamy Foster, *Marx's Ecology: Materialism and Nature* (New York: Monthly Review Press, 2000).

17 Cruikshank, *Do Glaciers Listen?,* 19–20.

BIBLIOGRAPHY

NEWSPAPERS

Calgary Daily Herald
The Daily Colonist (Vancouver, British Columbia)
The Denver Evening Post
Denver Tribune
Deseret Evening News (Salt Lake City, Utah)
Eastern Utah Advocate (Price, Utah)
Kootenay Mail (British Columbia)
Mail-Herald (Revelstoke, British Columbia)
New York Times
Ogden Standard Examiner (Utah)
Revelstoke Herald (British Columbia)
Salt Lake Daily Tribune
Salt Lake Daily Tribune and Utah Mining Gazette
San Juan (Silverton, Colorado)
San Juan Herald (Silverton, Colorado)
Seattle Daily Times
Silverton Democrat (Colorado)
Silverton Standard (Colorado)
Spokesman Review (Spokane, Washington)
Vancouver Daily Province (British Columbia)

MANUSCRIPT COLLECTIONS

Alfred E. Packer Collection, Stephen H. Hart Library, Colorado Historical Society, Denver.
Canadian Pacific Railway, Revelstoke Division Records, 1909–1975, Revelstoke Museum and Archives, Revelstoke, British Columbia.
Chappel Collection, Wenatchee Valley Museum and Archives, Wenatchee, Washington.

George A. Root Collection, Stephen H. Hart Library, Colorado Historical Society, Denver.

Railroad History File, Parks Canada Archives, Revelstoke, British Columbia.

Railway Slides File, Revelstoke Museum and Archives, Revelstoke, British Columbia.

Ruby El Hult Collection, Washington State University Library: Manuscripts, Archives, and Special Collections, Pullman, Washington.

Train Wrecks, Natural Disasters, and Snowslides File, Revelstoke Railway Museum, Revelstoke, British Columbia.

Transcript of Wellington Inquest, Robert Kelly, private collection, Renton, Washington.

Transcript of Testimony and Proceedings: *William Topping vs. G.N. Ry. Co.*, Records of State Supreme Court Case #11949, Washington State Archives, Olympia, Washington.

COURT CASES

Blythe et al. v. Denver and R. G. Ry. Co., 15 Colo. 339 (Colo. S. Ct. 1891).

Bowe v. Hunking, 135 Mass. 380 (Mass 1883).

Cormack v. New York N.H. and H.R.R. Co., 196 N.Y. 442 (N.Y. 1909)

Culshaw v. Crow's Nest Pass Coal Co. Ltd., 14 D.L.R. 25 (A.B. 1914).

Denver & R. G. R. Co. v. Andrews, 53 Pac. 518 (Colo. Ct. Appeals, 1898).

Denver & R. G. R. Co. v. Pilgrim, 47 Pac. 657 (Colo. Ct. Appeals, 1897).

Doyle v. Union Pacific Railway Co., 147 U.S. 413 (1893)

Gillespie v. St. Louis, K.C. & N.R. Co., 6 Mo. App. 554 (St. Louis Ct. of Appeals, 1879).

Jones v. Minneapolis & St. L. R. Co., 91 Minn. 229 (Minn. S. Ct., 1904).

Laidlaw v. Organ, 15 U.S. 178 (1817)

Lewinn v. Murphy, 63 Wash. 356 (Wash. S. Ct., 1911).

Lynch v. Ninemire Packing Co., 53 Wash. 423 (Wash. S. Ct. 1912).

Packer v. The People, 8 Colo. 361 (Colo. S. Ct., 1885).

Packer v. The People, 18 Colo. 525 (Colo. S. Ct., 1893).

Packer v. The People, 26 Colo. 306 (Colo. S. Ct., 1899).

William Topping, by guardian v. Great Northern Railway Co., Case No. 94511 (Sup. Ct. Wash.).

William Topping v. Great Northern Railway Co., 87 Wash. 702.

Woods v. Naumkeag Steam Cotton Co., 134 Mass. 357; s.c., 45 Am Rep. 344.

PRIMARY SOURCES

"A Colorado Tragedy." *Harper's Weekly* 18 (Oct. 17, 1874): 852.

Anderson, John. "Death Rode the Snows." *True West* 13 (Sept.–Oct. 1965): 44–45.

Bancroft, Hubert Howe. *History of Utah, 1540–1886*. San Francisco: History Co., 1889.

Breen, Patrick. *The Diary of Patrick Breen*. Edited by Kirsten Johnson. "New Light on the Donner Party," www.utahcrossroads.org/Donner Party/BreenDiary.html.

Bryant, Edwin. *What I Saw in California*, 4th ed. New York: Appleton & Co., 1849.

Calder, Donald G. Scott, "The Rogers Pass Snowslide," Sept. 1974, Railway Slides File, Revelstoke Museum and Archives, Revelstoke, B.C.

Clarke, F. L. "Caught in a Sierra Nevada Snow-Storm." *Overland Monthly* 11, no. 65 (May 1888): 512–16.

Clayton, William. *The Latter-Day Saints' Emigrants' Guide*. St. Louis, Republican Steam Power Press-Chambers and Knapp, 1848.

Clyman, James. *Journal of a Mountain Man*. Edited by Linda M. Hasselstrom. Missoula, Mont.: Mountain Press, 1984.

"The Colorado Disaster." *Harper's Weekly: Journal of Civilization* 28, no. 1417 (Feb. 16, 1884): 111.

Dimock, A. W. "Adventures on Skees and Snowshoes." *Country Life in America* (Dec. mid-month, 1910): 185–88.

Doten, Carroll. "Recent Railway Accidents in the United States." *Publications of the American Statistical Association* 9, no. 69 (March 1905): 155–81.

Dugmore, A. Radclyffe. "Camping in the Snow." *Country Life in America* 3 (Jan. 1903): 111–14.

Dyer, John L. *The Snow-Shoe Itinerant: An Autobiography*. Cincinnati: Cranston and Stowe, 1890.

Ferris, Warren A. *Life in the Rocky Mountains: A Diary of Wanderings on the Sources of the Rivers Missouri, Columbia, and Colorado from February, 1830, to November, 1835*, edited by Paul C. Phillips. Denver: F. A. Rosenstock, Old West Publishing, 1940.

Frémont, John C. *The Expeditions of John C. Frémont, Volume 3, 1848–1854*. Edited by Donald Jackson and Mary Lee Spence. Urbana and Chicago: University of Illinois Press, 1984.

Gardiner, Charles Fox. *Doctor at Timberline*. Caldwell, Idaho: Caxton Printers, 1938.

Gibbons, J. J. *In the San Juan, Colorado: Sketches*. Chicago: Calumet Book and Engraving Co., 1898.

Goodwin, J. M. "The Prospector." *Overland Monthly* 34 (Aug. 1899): 160–65.

Goodwin, J. M. "Snowslides in the Rockies; A Perilous Study." *Overland Monthly* 29 (April 1897), 381–85.

Hastings, James K. "A Winter in the High Mountains, 1871–72." *Colorado Magazine* (July 1950), 225–34.

Hastings, Lansford W. *Emigrants' Guide to Oregon and California*. Cincinnati: Published by George Conclin, 1845.

Hawley, H. J. "H. J. Hawley's Diary, Russell Gulch in 1860." Edited by Lynn I. Perrigo. *Colorado Magazine* 31 (Oct. 1954): 133–49.

Howard, Merridan. "How Railway Men Fight Snow." *Pearson's Magazine* 5 (Jan. to June, 1898): 26–34.

"In the San Juan." *Harper's Weekly* 27 (June 9, 1883): 365.

"The Luck of LaChance." Transcript. CBC interview, 1979, Railroad History File, Parks Canada, Revelstoke, British Columbia.

Lynde, F. "How the Railroads Fight Snow." *Munsey's Magazine* 22 (Oct. 1899–March 1900): 478–486.

McIlwraith, Jean N. "Winter Sports, Old and New." *Country Life in America* (Dec. 1905): 175–187.

Mills, Enos A. "A Home of Forest Fire Logs." *Sunset* 46, no. 5 (May 1921): 66–68.

———. "Being Nice to Skunks." *Sunset* 48, no. 1 (Jan. 1922): 49–50.

———. "Dangers of Snowslides." *Harper's Weekly* 48 (1904).

———. "Grizzly's High-Power Nose." *Atlantic Monthly* (Jan. 1922): 36

———. "Little Blue." *Sunset* 52, no. 1 (Jan. 1924): 47–48, 60.

———. "Racing an Avalanche." *Country Life* 19 (1910): 39–44.

———. "Rescuing Her Cub." *Atlantic Monthly* (Oct. 1922): 527.

———. *Rocky Mountain Wonderland*. Boston: Houghton Mifflin, 1915.

———. "Snow-Blinded on the Summit." *New Country Life* 33 (1918): 41–44.

———. "Snowflake and Snowslide." *Independent* 70 (1911): 1316–18.

———. "The Story of a Thousand Year Pine." *Atlantic Monthly* (Dec. 1914): 59

———. "Wild Animal Homesteads." *Sunset* 50, no. 1 (Jan. 1923): 45–47, 58.

Mitchell, Guy Elliot. "Landslides and Rock Avalanches." *National Geographic Magazine* 21 (April 1910): 287.

Muir, John. *The Mountains of California*. New York: Century, 1901.

———. *Stickeen*. Berkeley: Heyday Books, 1990 (reprinted from Houghton Mifflin, 1909).

"Nose-Blackening as Preventive of Snow-Blindness." *Nature* 38 (May 3, 1888): 7.

"Nose-Blackening as Preventive of Snow-Blindness." *Nature* 38 (May 31, 1888): 101–102.

"Nose-Blackening as Preventive of Snow-Blindness." *Nature* 38 (June 21, 1888): 172.

"Nose-Blackening as Preventive of Snow-Blindness." *Nature* 40 (Sept. 5, 1889): 438.

Palmer, Greville. "'Snow Bucking' in the Rocky Mountains." *Longman's Magazine* 5 (Feb. 1885), 422–31.

Pritchett, Lulita Crawford, *Diary of Lulie Margie Crawford: A Little Girl's View of Life in the Old West, 1880–1881*. Denver: Egan, 1985.

Roosevelt, Theodore. *The Works of Theodore Roosevelt in Fourteen Volumes: The Strenuous Life*. New York: P. F. Collier and Son, 1900.

Russell, Osborne. *Journal of a Trapper*. Lincoln: University of Nebraska Press, 1986.

Ruxton, A. F. *Adventures in Mexico and the Rocky Mountains*. Glorieta, N.M.: Rio Grande Press, 1973.

Spearman, Frank H. "Sankey's Double-Header." *McClure's Magazine* 14 (March 1900): 456–66.

Squier, H. G. "The Snow-Shoers of Plumas," *California Illustrated Magazine, 1891* (Feb. 1894): 318–24.

Thoreau, Henry David, "The Maine Woods." Edited by William Howarth. *Thoreau in the Mountains: Writings by Henry David Thoreau*. New York: Farrar, Straus, Giroux, 1982.

United States Reports, Vol. 147. New York: Banks and Brothers, Law Publishers, 1893.

U.S. Census, 1890 and 1900.

Warman, Cy. "The Battle of the Snow-Plows. A True Story of Railroading in the Rocky Mountains." *McClure's Magazine* 8 (Nov. 1896): 92–96.

Warren, E. R. "Snow-Shoeing in the Rocky Mountains." *Outing Magazine* 9 (Jan. 1887): 352.

Washington Reports, Vol. 81. "Cases Determined in the Supreme Court of Washington, 1 August 1914–26 September 1914." Seattle and San Francisco: Bancroft-Whitney, 1915.

Wason, H. L. "The Slide at the Empire Mine," *Letters from Colorado*. Boston: Cupples and Hurd, 1887, 154–56.

Willey, Day Allen. "Rocky Mountain Avalanches." *Scientific American* 92 (Feb. 25, 1905): 164–66.

Wister, Owen. *The Virginian*. New York: Signet Classic, 2002.

Young, Winthrop Geoffrey. *Mountain Craft*. New York: Scribner's Sons, 1920.

SECONDARY SOURCES

Abbott, Carl, Stephen J. Leonard, and David McComb. *Colorado: A History of the Centennial State*. Niwot: University of Colorado Press, 1994.

Allen, E. John B. "Skiing Mailmen of Mountain America: U.S. Winter Postal Service in the Nineteenth Century," *Journal of the West* 29 (1990): 76–86.

Anderson, John. "Death Rode the Snows," *True West* 12 (Sept.–Oct. 1965): 44–45, 62–63.

Anderson, William M., Dale L. Morgan, and Eleanor T. Harris. *The Rocky Mountain Journals of William Marshall Anderson: The West in 1834*. San Marino, Calif.: Huntington Library, 1967.

Andrews, Thomas G. *Killing for Coal: America's Deadliest Labor War*. Cambridge: Harvard University Press, 2008.

———. "'Made by Toile?' Tourism, Labor, and the Construction of the Colorado Landscape, 1858–1917." *Journal of American History* 92 (Dec. 2005): 837–63.

———. "The Road to Ludlow: Work, Environment, and Industrialization, 1870–1915," PhD dissertation, University of Wisconsin, 2003.

Armstrong, Betsy R. *Century of Struggle Against Snow: A History of Avalanche Hazard in San Juan County, Colorado.* Boulder, Colo.: Institute of Arctic and Alpine Research, occasional paper, 1976.

Armstrong, Betsy R., and Knox Williams. *The Avalanche Book.* Golden, Colo.: Fulcrum, 1992.

Arrington, Leonard. "Abundance from the Earth: The Beginnings of Commercial Mining in Utah." *Utah Historical Quarterly* 31 (Summer 1963): 192–219.

Arrington, Leonard J., and Davis Bitton. *The Mormon Experience: A History of the Latter-day Saints.* Urbana: University of Illinois Press, 1992.

Athearn, Robert G. *The Mythic West in Twentieth-Century America.* Lawrence: University of Kansas Press, 1986.

Backler, Gary G. "The C.P.R.'s Capacity and Investment Strategy in Rogers Pass, B.C., 1882–1916," master's thesis, University of British Columbia, 1981.

Backler, Gary G., and Treavor D. Heaver. "The Timing of a Major Investment in Railway Capacity: CPR's Connaught Tunnel Decision." *Business History* 24 (Fall 1982): 300–14.

Bakken, Gordon Morris. *The Development of Law on the Rocky Mountain Frontier: Civil Law and Society, 1850–1912* .Westport, Conn.: Westport Press, 1983.

Beck, Ulrich. *Ecological Enlightenment: Essays on the Politics of the Risk Society.* Atlantic Highlands, N.J.: Humanities Press, 1995.

———. *Risk Society: Towards a New Modernity.* London and Newbury Park, Calif.: Sage, 1992.

Beck, Ulrich, Anthony Giddens, and Scott Lasht. *Reflexive Modernization: Politics, Tradition and Aesthetics in the Modern Social Order.* Oxford: Blackwell Press, 1994.

Beckey, Fred. *Range of Glaciers: The Exploration and Survey of the Northern Cascade Range.* Portland: Oregon Historical Society Press, 2003.

Belk, Russell W., and Janeen Arnold Costa. "The Mountain Man Myth: A Contemporary Consuming Fantasy." *Journal of Consumer Research* 25 (Dec. 1998): 218–40.

Benson, Jack A. "Before Skiing Was Fun." *Western Historical Quarterly* 8 (Oct. 1997): 431–42.

Bernier, Ivan, and Andree LaJoie, eds. *Law, Society, and the Economy.* Toronto: University of Toronto Press, 1986.

Billington, Ray A. *America's Frontier Culture: Three Essays.* College Station: Texas A&M University Press, 1977.

———. "Books That Won the West: The Guidebooks of the Forty-Niners and Fifty-Niners." *American West* 4, no. 3 (Aug. 1967): 25–32, 72–75.

Boag, Peter. *Environment and Experience: Settlement Culture in Nineteenth-Century Oregon.* Berkeley: University of California Press, 1992.

————. "Overlanders and the Snake River Region: A Case Study of Landscape Perception in the Early Northwest." *Pacific Northwest Quarterly* 84, no. 4 (Oct. 1993): 122–29.

Bonnemaison, Joël, *Culture and Space: Conceiving a New Cultural Geography.* London and New York: I. B. Tauris, 2005.

Bowman, Anthony Will. "From Silver to Skis: A History of Alta, Utah, and Little Cottonwood Canyon, 1847–1966," master's thesis, Utah State University, 1967.

Bramwell, Lincoln. "Natural Bonanza: Environment and Economy in Park City, Utah." Presentation, American Society of Environmental Historians' Conference, Denver, Colorado, Feb. 12–15, 2002.

Brosnan, Kathleen A. *Uniting Mountain and Plain: Cities, Law, and Environmental Change Along the Front Range.* Albuquerque: University of New Mexico Press, 2002.

Brown, Robert L. *An Empire of Silver: A History of the San Juan Silver Rush.* Caldwell, Idaho: Caxton Printers, 1965.

————. *Ghost Towns of the Colorado Rockies.* Caldwell, Idaho: Caxton Printers, 1968.

Buckley, Karen. *Danger, Death, and Disaster in the Crowsnest Pass Mines, 1902–1928.* Calgary: University of Calgary Press, 2004.

Burton, Ian, Robert W. Kates, and Gilbert F. White, eds. *The Environment as Hazard.* New York: Guilford Press, 1993.

Careless, J. M. *Frontier and Metropolis: Regions, Cities, and Identities in Canada before 1914.* Toronto: University of Toronto Press, 1989.

Carter, Harvey L., and Marcia C. Spencer. "Stereotypes of the Mountain Man." *Western Historical Quarterly* 6 (Jan. 1975): 17–32.

Chaffin, Tom. *Pathfinder: John Charles Frémont and the Course of American Empire.* New York: Hill and Wang, 2002.

Clark, Cecil, "Disaster at Avalanche Mountain," *Daily Colonist* (Victoria, B.C.), Nov. 15, 1959.

Clokey, Richard M. *William H. Ashley: Enterprise and Politics in the Trans-Mississippi West.* Norman: University of Oklahoma Press, 1980.

Coleman, Annie G. *Ski Style: Sport and Culture in the Rockies.* Lawrence: University Press of Kansas, 2004.

Cronon, William. *Changes in the Land: Indians, Colonists, and the Ecology of New England.* New York: Hill and Wang, 1983.

————. *Nature's Metropolis: Chicago and the Great West.* New York: W. W. Norton, 1991.

————, ed. *Uncommon Ground: Rethinking the Human Place in Nature.* New York: W. W. Norton, 1996.

Cronon, William, George Miles, and Jay Gitlin, eds. *Under an Open Sky: Rethinking America's Western Past.* New York: W. W. Norton, 1992.

Crum, Josie Moore. "The San Juan Country." In *Pioneers of the San Juan*, Vol. 1, Sarah Platt Decker Chapter of the D.A.R. Colorado Springs: Out West Printing and Stationery Co., 1942.

Cutter, Susan L., ed. *American Hazardscapes: The Regionalization of Hazards and Disasters*. Washington, D.C.: Joseph Henry Press, 2001.

Deverell, William, ed. *A Companion to the American West*. Malden, Mass.: Blackwell, 2004.

Di Stefano, Diana L. "Alfred Packer's World: Risk, Responsibility and the Place of Experience in Mountain Culture, 1873–1907." *Journal of Social History* 40 (Fall 2006): 181–204.

Dorset, Phyllis Flanders. *The Story of Colorado's Gold and Silver Rushes*. New York: Barnes and Noble Books, 1994.

Dynes, Russell R., and Kathleen J. Tierney, eds. *Disasters, Collective Behavior, and Social Organization*. Newark: University of Delaware Press, 1994.

El Hult, Ruby. *Northwest Disaster: Avalanche and Fire*. Portland, Oreg.: Binford and Mort, 1960.

Ely, James W. *Railroads and American Law*. Lawrence: University Press of Kansas, 2001.

Emmons, David. *The Butte Irish: Class and Ethnicity in an American Mining Town, 1875–1925*. Urbana: University of Illinois Press, 1990.

English, Cathy. "Research Report Regarding the Snowslide at Rogers Pass, March 4th, 1910." Railway Slides File, Revelstoke Museum and Archives, Revelstoke, British Columbia.

Enyeart, John P. "By Laws of Their Own Making: Political Culture and the Everyday Politics of the Mountain West Working Class, 1870–1917," PhD dissertation, University of Colorado, Boulder, 2002.

Etulain, Richard W. *Beyond the Missouri: The Story of the American West*. Albuquerque: University of New Mexico Press, 2006.

———, ed. *Does the Frontier Experience Make America Exceptional?* Bedford, Mass.: St. Martin's Press, 1999.

Faragher, John Mack, ed. *Rereading Frederick Jackson Turner: "The Significance of the Frontier in American History" and Other Essays*. New York: Henry Holt, 1994.

Fay, Abbot. *Ski Tracks in the Rockies: A Century of Colorado Skiing*. Louisville, Colo.: Cordillera Press, 1984.

Flores, Dan. *The Natural West: Environmental History in the Great Plains and Rocky Mountains*. Norman: University of Oklahoma Press, 2001.

———. "Place: An Argument for Bioregional History." *Environmental History Review* 18 (Winter 1994): 1–18.

Fraser, Colin. *Avalanches and Snow Safety*. London: John Murray, 1978.

Friedman, Lawrence. *A History of American Law*. New York: Simon & Schuster, 1985.

Friedman, Lawrence M., and Jack Ladinsky. "Social Change and the Law of Industrial Accidents." *Columbia Law Review* 67 (Jan. 1967): 50–82.

Gantt, Paul H. *The Case of Alfred Packer, the Man-Eater.* Denver: University of Denver Press, 1952.

Giddens, Anthony. "Risk and Responsibility." *Modern Law Review* 62 (Jan. 1999): 1–10.

Goodman, Nan. *Shifting the Blame: Literature, Law, and the Theory of Accidents in Nineteenth-Century America.* New York: Routledge, 1998.

Gordon, Sarah Barringer. "Law and the Contact of Cultures." In *A Companion to the American West.* Edited by William Deverell. Malden, Mass. Blackwell, 2004, 130–142.

Grayson, Donald. "The Donner Party: Sex and Death on the Western Immigrant Trail." *Inside Chico State* 31, no. 15 (April 26, 2001), www.csuchico.edu/pub/inside/archive/01_04_26/02.donnerparty. html.

Hodges, Joseph G. "The Legal Experiences of Mr. Alfred Packer." *Dicta* 19 (June 1942): 149–54.

Hoganson, Kirsten L. *Fighting for American Manhood: How Gender Politics Provoked the Spanish-American and Philippine-American Wars.* New Haven: Yale University Press, 1998.

Horwitz, Morton J. *The Transformation of American Law, 1870–1960: The Crisis of Legal Orthodoxy.* Oxford: Oxford University Press, 1992.

Hyde, Anne F. "Round Pegs in Square Holes: The Rocky Mountains and Extractive Industry." In *Many Wests: Place, Culture, and Regional Identity.* Edited by David M. Wrobel and Michael C. Steiner. Lawrence: University of Kansas Press, 1997, 93–113.

———. "Transients and Stickers: The Problem of Community in the American West." In *A Companion Reader to the American West.* Edited by William Deverell. Malden, Mass.: Blackwell, 2004, 304–28.

Igler, David. *Industrial Cowboys: Miller & Lux and the Transformation of the Far West, 1850–1920.* Berkeley: University of California Press, 2001.

Irving, Washington, and Benjamin L. E. de Bonneville. *The Adventures of Captain Bonneville.* Boston: Twayne, 1977.

Jacobs, Pat. *Mountain Madman or Mountain Madness?* Lake City, Colo.: Pat Jacobs, 1965.

Jacoby, Karl. *Crimes against Nature: Squatters, Poachers, Thieves, and the Hidden History of American Conservation.* Berkeley: University of California Press, 2001.

Jameson, Elizabeth. *All That Glitters: Class, Conflict, and Community in Cripple Creek.* Urbana: University of Illinois Press, 1998.

Jameson, Elizabeth, and Susan Armitage, eds. *Writing the Range: Race, Class, and Culture in the Women's West.* Norman: University of Oklahoma Press, 1997.

Jenkins, John W. *Colorado Avalanche Disasters: An Untold Story of the Old West.* Ouray, Colo.: Western Reflections, 2001.

Jenkins, McKay. *The White Death: Tragedy and Heroism in the Avalanche Zone.* New York: Random House, 2000.

Johnson, Susan Lee. *Roaring Camp: The Social World of the California Gold Rush.* New York, W. W. Norton, 2000.

Kazis, Richard. *Fear at Work: Job Blackmail, Labor, and the Environment.* New York: Pilgrim Press, 1982.

Keller, Charles L. *The Lady in the Ore Bucket: A History of Settlement and Industry in the Tri-Canyon Area of the Wasatch Mountains.* Salt Lake City: University of Utah Press, 2001.

Kern, Stephen. *The Culture of Time and Space, 1880–1918.* Cambridge: Harvard University Press, 1983.

Kramer, Stephen. *Avalanche.* Minneapolis: Carolihoda Books, 1992.

Krist, Gary. *The White Cascade: The Great Northern Railway Disaster and America's Deadliest Avalanche.* New York: Henry Holt, 2007.

Kristin, Johnson, ed. *Unfortunate Emigrants: Narratives of the Donner Party.* Logan, Utah: Utah State University Press, 1996.

Kushner, Ervan F. *Alfred G. Packer: Cannibal! Victim?* Frederick, Colo.: Platte 'N Press, 1980.

LaFollette, Marcel C. *Making Science Our Own: Public Images of Science, 1910–1955.* Chicago: University of Chicago Press, 1990.

Lears, T. J. Jackson. *Fables of Abundance: A Cultural History of Advertising in America.* New York: Basic Books, 1994.

———. *No Place of Grace: Antimodernism and the Transformation of American Culture, 1880–1920.* Chicago: University of Chicago Press, 1994.

Limerick, Patricia Nelson. *The Legacy of Conquest: The Unbroken Past of the American West.* New York: W. W. Norton, 1987.

Limerick, Patricia Nelson, Clyde A. Milner II, and Charles E. Rankin, eds., *Trails: Towards a New Western History.* Lawrence: University Press of Kansas, 1991.

Lingenfelter, Richard E. *The Hardrock Miners: A History of the Mining Labor Movement in the American West, 1863–1893* Berkeley: University of California Press, 1974.

Lipset, Seymour Martin. *Continental Divide: The Values and Institutions of the United States and Canada.* Middletown, Conn.: Wesleyan University Press, 1982.

Lower, J. Arthur. *Western Canada: An Outline History.* Vancouver: Douglas and McIntyre, 1983.

Mann, Ralph. *After the Gold Rush: Society in Grass Valley and Nevada City, California, 1849–1870.* Stanford: Stanford University Press, 1982.

Marsh, Kevin R. "The Ups and Downs of Mountain Life: Historical Patterns of

Adaptation in the Cascade Mountains." *Western Historical Quarterly* 35 (Summer 2004): 193–213.

Mazzulla, Fred, and Jo Mazzulla. *Al Packer: A Colorado Cannibal.* Denver: Fred and Jo Mazulla, 1968.

McDowell, Andrea G. "From Commons to Claims: Property Rights in the California Gold Rush." *Yale Journal of Law and the Humanities* 12 (Winter 2002): 1–72.

McEvoy, Arthur F. *The Fisherman's Problem: Ecology and Law in the California Fisheries, 1850–1980.* New York: Cambridge University Press, 1986.

McGrath, Roger D. *Gunfighters, Highwaymen, and Vigilantes: Violence on the Frontier.* Berkeley: University of California Press, 1984.

Merchant, Carolyn. *Ecological Revolutions: Nature, Gender, and Science in New England.* Chapel Hill: University of North Carolina Press, 1989.

Mercier, Laurie. *Anaconda: Labor, Community, and Culture in Montana's Smelter City.* Urbana: University of Illinois Press, 2001.

Montgomery, David. *Citizen Workers: The Experience of Workers in the United States with Democracy and the Free Market During the Nineteenth Century.* Cambridge: Cambridge University Press, 1993.

———. *The Fall of the House of Labor.* Cambridge: Cambridge University Press, 1987.

———. "Workers' Control of Machine Production in the Nineteenth Century." *Labor History* 17 (Fall 1976): 485–509.

Moody, Don. *America's Worst Train Disaster: The 1910 Wellington Tragedy.* Plano, Tex.: Abique, 1998.

Morse, Kathryn. *The Nature of Gold: An Environmental History of the Klondike Gold Rush.* Seattle: University of Washington Press, 2003.

Moses, Albert L. "Judge Gerry's Sentence of Alfred Packer." *Dicta* 19 (1942): 169–71.

Mouat, Jeremy. *Roaring Days: Rossland's Mines and the History of British Columbia.* Vancouver: University of British Columbia Press, 1995.

Murphy, Mary. *Mining Cultures: Men, Women, and Leisure in Butte, 1914–41.* Urbana: University of Illinois Press, 1997.

Nash, Roderick. *Wilderness and the American Mind.* New Haven: Yale University Press, 1982.

Nicolson, Marjorie Hope. *Mountain Gloom and Mountain Glory: The Development of the Aesthetic of the Infinite.* Cornell: Cornell University Press, 1959.

Nobbs, Ruby. *Rail Tales from the Revelstoke Division.* Altona, Manitoba: Friesens, 2000.

Oman, Kerry R. "Winter in the Rockies: Winter Quarters of the Mountain Men," *Montana: The Magazine of Western History* 52, no. 1 (Spring 2002): 34–47.

Owens, Kenneth N. "The Mormon-Carson Emigrant Trail in Western History." *Montana: The Magazine of Western History* (42 Winter 1992): 14–25.

Peck, Gunther. "Manly Gambles: The Politics of Risk on the Comstock Lode." *Journal of Social History* 26 (Summer 1993): 701–23.

———. *Reinventing Free Labor: Padrones and Immigrant Workers in the North American West, 1880–1930.* Cambridge: Cambridge University Press, 2000.

Pellow, David Naguib. *Garbage Wars: The Struggle for Environmental Justice in Chicago (Urban and Industrial Environments).* Cambridge: MIT Press, 2004.

Pidgeon, Nick. "Safety Culture and Risk Management in Organizations." *Journal of Cross-Cultural Psychology* 22, no. 1 (March 1991): 129–40.

Pomeroy, Earl. *In Search of the Golden West: The Tourist in Western America.* New York: Alfred A. Knopf, 1957.

———. "Toward a Reorientation of Western History: Continuity and Environment." *Mississippi Valley Historical Review* 41, no. 4 (March 1955): 579–600.

Poor, M. C. *Denver, South Park and Pacific.* Denver: Rocky Mountain Railroad Club, 1976.

Pugsley, Edmund E. "Some Had Luck." *Railroad Magazine* 48 (Feb. 1949): 70–78.

Pyne, Stephen J. *Year of the Fires.* New York: Penguin Books, 2001.

Reid, John Phillip. *Law for the Elephant: Property and Social Behavior on the Overland Trail.* San Marino, Calif.: Huntington Library, 1980.

———. "The Layers of Western Legal History." In *Law for the Elephant, Law for the Beaver: Essays in the Legal History of the North American West.* Edited by John McLaren, Hamar Foster, and Chet Orloff. Pasadena, Calif.: Ninth Judicial Circuit Historical Society, 1992.

Robbins, William G. *Colony and Empire: The Capitalist Transformation of the American West.* Lawrence: University of Kansas Press, 1994.

Robertson, Ruth Winder. *This Is Alta.* Ruth W. Robertson, 1972.

Rothman, Hal K. *Devil's Bargains: Tourism in the Twentieth-Century American West.* Lawrence: University Press of Kansas, 2000.

Rotundo, Anthony E. *American Manhood: Transformations in Masculinity from the Revolution to the Modern Era.* New York: Basic Books, 1993.

Runte, Alfred. *National Parks: The American Experience.* 3rd ed. Lincoln: University of Nebraska Press, 1997.

Russell, Carl P. *Firearms, Traps, and Tools of the Mountain Men.* New York: Knopf, 1967.

Sarat, Austin, Lawrence Douglas, and Martha Merrill Umphrey, eds. *The Place of Law.* Ann Arbor: University of Michigan Press, 2003.

Schivelbusch, Wolfgang. *The Railway Journey: Industrialization of Time and Space in the 19th Century.* Berkeley: University of California Press, 1977.

Schrepfer, Susan R. *Nature's Altars: Mountains, Gender, and American Environmentalism.* Lawrence: University of Kansas Press, 2005.

Schwantes, Carlos A. *Radical Heritage: Labor, Socialism, and Reform in Washington and British Columbia, 1885–1917.* Moscow: University of Idaho Press, 1994.

Sharp, Paul. *Whoop-Up Country: The Canadian and American West, 1865–1885.* Minneapolis: University of Minnesota Press, 1955.

Shugerman, Jed Handelsman. "The Floodgates of Strict Liability: Bursting Reservoirs and the Adoption of *Fletcher v. Rylands* in the Gilded Age." *Yale Law Journal* 110, no. 2 (Nov. 2000): 333–77.

Simpson, A. W. Brian. *Cannibalism and the Common Law: The Story of the Tragic Last Voyage of the* Mignonette *and the Strange Legal Proceedings to Which It Gave Rise.* Chicago: University of Chicago Press, 1984.

Spetz, Steven N. *Canadian Criminal Law.* Toronto: Sir Isaac Pitman, 1972.

Spurr, Wendy, and Kimberly Spurr. *Alfred Packer's High Protein Cookbook.* Grand Junction, Colo.: Centennial, 1995.

Steinberg, Ted. *Acts of God: the Unnatural History of Natural Disasters in America.* Oxford: Oxford University Press, 2000.

Stewart, George R. *Ordeal by Hunger: The Story of the Donner Party.* Lincoln and London: University of Nebraska Press, 1936.

Stromquist, Shelton. *A Generation of Boomers: The Pattern of Railroad Labor Conflict in Nineteenth-Century America.* Urbana: University of Illinois Press, 1993.

Swagerty, William R. "Marriage and Settlement Patterns of Rocky Mountain Trappers and Traders." *Western Historical Quarterly* 11 (April 1980): 159–80.

Takaki, Ronald. *Strangers from a Different Shore: A History of Asian Americans.* Boston: Little, Brown, 1989.

Thompson, E. P. *The Making of the English Working Class.* New York: Vintage Books, 1963.

———. *Whigs and Hunters: The Origin of the Black Act.* London: Allen Lane, 1975.

Thornton, J. Quinn. *Oregon and California in 1848.* In *Unfortunate Emigrants: Narratives of the Donner Party.* Edited by Kristin Johnson. Logan: Utah State University Press, 1996.

Tierney, Kathleen J. "Toward a Critical Sociology of Risk," *Sociological Forum* 14 (June 1999): 215–42.

Trennert, Robert A. *Riding the High Wire: Aerial Tramways in the West.* Boulder: University of Colorado Press, 2001.

Tuan, Yi-Fu. *Topophilia: A Study of Environmental Perceptions, Attitudes, and Values.* Englewood Cliffs, N.J.: Prentice Hall, 1974.

Tucker, Robert C. *The Marx-Engels Reader.* New York: W. W. Norton, 1972.

Turner, Barry A., and Nick F. Pidgeon. *Man-Made Disasters.* Oxford: Butterworth-Heinemann, 1978.

Turner, Frederick Jackson. "The Significance of the Frontier in American History." *Annual Report of the American Historical Association for the Year 1893.*

Washington, D.C.: Government Publishing Office and American Historical Association, 1894, 199–277.

Unruh, John D., Jr. *The Plains Across: The Overland Emigrants and the Trans-Mississippi West, 1840–1860.* Urbana: University of Illinois Press, 1979.

Van Kirk, Sylvia. *Many Tender Ties: Women in Fur-Trade Society, 1670–1870.* Norman: University of Oklahoma Press, 1983.

Vestal, Stanley. *Jim Bridger, Mountain Man: A Biography.* New York: Morrow, 1946.

Warren, Louis S. *The Hunter's Game: Poachers and Conservationists in Twentieth-Century America.* New Haven: Yale University Press, 1997.

Webb, Walter Prescott. *The Great Plains.* Lincoln: University of Nebraska Press, 1931.

Westrup, Hugh. "Avalanche!" *Current Science* 83 (Dec. 12, 1997): 10.

Whelan, John. "Frozen Hell on Earth." *Mountain Heritage Magazine: The Journal of Rocky Mountain Life and History* 3 (Winter 2000/2001): 12–16.

White, Richard. "Are You an Environmentalist, or Do You Work for a Living?" In *Uncommon Ground.* Edited by William Cronon. New York: W. W. Norton, 1996, 171–85.

———. *"It's Your Misfortune and None of My Own": A History of the American West.* Norman: University of Oklahoma Press, 1991.

———. *Land Use, Environment, and Social Change: The Shaping of Island County, Washington.* Seattle: University of Washington Press, 1980.

———. *The Organic Machine: The Remaking of the Columbia River.* New York: Hill and Wang, 1995.

Williams-Searle, John. "Courting Risk: Disability, Masculinity, and Liability on Iowa's Railroads, 1868–1900." *Annals of Iowa* 58 (Winter 1999): 24–77.

Wilson, Elinor. *Jim Beckwourth: Black Mountain Man and War Chief of the Crows.* Norman: University of Oklahoma Press, 1972.

Wisner, Ben, Piers Blaikie, Terry Cannon, and Ian Davis, eds. *At Risk: Natural Hazards, People's Vulnerability and Disasters,* 2nd ed. London: Routledge, 1994.

Woods, John G. *Snow War: An Illustrated History of Rogers Pass, Glacier National Park, B.C.* Edited by John S. Marsh. Ottawa: NPPAC, Canada, 1983.

Worster, Donald. *Rivers of Empire: Water, Aridity, and the Growth of the American West.* New York: Oxford University Press, 1985.

Wrobel, David, and Michael C. Steiner, eds. *Many Wests: Place, Culture, and Regional Identity.* Lawrence: University of Kansas Press, 1997.

Wyman, Mark. *Hard Rock Epic: Western Miners and the Industrial Revolution, 1860–1910.* Berkeley: University of California Press, 1979.

———. "Industrial Revolution in the West: Hard-Rock Miners and the New Technology," *Western Historical Quarterly* 5, no. 1 (Jan. 1974): 39–57.

Zhu, Liping. *A Chinaman's Chance: The Chinese on the Rocky Mountain Mining Frontier.* Niwot: University Press of Colorado, 1997.

———. "'A Chinaman's Chance' on the Rocky Mountain Mining Frontier." *Montana: The Magazine of* Western History 45, no. 4 (Autumn/Winter 1995): 36–51.

———. "No Need to Rush: The Chinese, Placer Mining, and the Western Environment." *Montana: The Magazine of Western History* 49, no. 3 (Autumn 1999): 42–57.

Zinn, Howard *A People's History of the United States.* New York: Harper Perennial, 1980.

INDEX

mining, 38–42; and building community, 42–49; corporate, 38–39; gold, 6, 33, 38, 47 (*see also* gold); silver, 6, 24, 38, 39, 42, 44, 47

Moffatt, James, 67–68, 71–72, 86

Monroe, Jack, 35–36

Mountain West, shared experiences in, 49–52

Murray, Eli, 47

Northern Pacific Railway (NP), 57

Norwegians, 32–33

O'Neill, James H., 92, 95–96, 105, 114; electrical storm and, 100; Henry White and, 92, 93, 106; John Merritt and, 91; refusal to increase wages, 98, 102; testimony, 95–98

Peck, Gunther, 49–50

Penrose, Charles, 45–46

Perley, E. W., 100–101

Pettit, Joseph L., 91, 103

Pilgrim, Christopher A., 75

Plumas, California, 31

postal carriers, 28–31

priests and preachers, 32–33, 37

Procunier, Charles, 63

rail lines, snow problems on, 55–58

railway accidents, 58

railway workers, 53–55, 59–60, 102; experienced workers, risk, and disaster, 65–67; heroic efforts to keep tracks clear, 53–54; seasonal, 58, 67, 74; and snow problems on rail lines, 55–58; temporary, 67–69, 73. *See also* Canadian Pacific Railway; Wellington avalanche

Raines, J. A., 119

Rainier, Mount, 5

Reed, James, 21

rescues and rescue services, 45–49, 63, 65–66, 77, 120. *See also* Canadian Pacific Railway

Revelstoke, British Columbia, 60–62

Rocky Mountain Fur Company, 16

Rogers, Albert Bowan, 57

Rogers, John F., 94, 95

Rogers Pass, 56, 60–63, 66, 68, 70

Rogers Pass avalanche of 1910 (Rogers Pass slide), 63–65, 68, 73, 85, 87; community response and questions of responsibility, 69–74; company response in Revelstoke, 85–88. *See also* Canadian Pacific Railway

Rogers Pass station, 60–61

Rogers Pass Tunnel, 122

Ross, James, 56

rotary plow, 58

Russell, Osborne, 12–13, 15, 16

Ryan, Pat, 98

Salt Lake City, 21–22, 46–47

San Juan Country, 23–24, 26

San Juan County, 38–39

San Juan Mountains, 5, 43

Sargent, Lewis, 33–34

Scenic, 91, 92, 94, 107, 114

search-and-rescue operations. *See* rescues and rescue services

Selkirk Mountains, 56, 57, 60, 63. *See also* Revelstoke

Shaughnessy, Thomas, 70–71

Sherlock, Basil, 105

Shugerman, Jed, 118

Sierra Nevada, 5

silver, 5–6, 24, 47

silver mining, 6, 24, 38, 39, 42, 44, 47. *See also* mining